Rhythm n' Typing

1ˢᵗ Edition

Teach Yourself How To Type

**All Laid Out For You • Easy To Follow
Very Effortless • Very Effective**

Dino Greco - Alex Greco - Marcia Tsuchiya - Tony Greco

Rhythm n' Typing

25 <u>Rhythmical</u> easy typing lessons for the starting to efficient level typist of any age.

This book's concept is exclusively based on the use of rhyming sets of words of 4 letters typed with rhythm all organized into 25 lessons.

The 4 letter words concept is a smart approach to typing considering that around 65% of all commonly used words are made up of 4 letters or less.

Rhythm n' Typing is great for self teaching typing at any age and excellent in any learning setting.

First Edition

Copyright © 2013 Dino Greco, Alex Greco, Marcia Tsuchiya, Tony Greco

ALL RIGHTS RESERVED. No part of this work covered by the copyright herein may be reproduced, transmitted, or used in any form or by any means, graphic, electronic, or mechanical, including photocopying, recording, taping, Web distribution, or by any information storage or retrieval systems without the prior written permission of the publisher which represents the interest of the authors.

ISBN: 1494496658
ISBN-13: 978-1494496654
Library of Congress Control Number: 2014906803

Some people dream of success... while others wake up and work hard at it.

— Author Unknown

Be not afraid of going slowly; be afraid only of standing still.

— Chinese Proverb

Never put off for tomorrow, what you can do today.

— Thomas Jefferson

A water drop hollows a stone.

— Ovid

Practice does not make perfect. Only perfect practice makes perfect.

— Vince Lombardi

The distance extinguishes the small fires but raises the bigger ones. Dedicated to our grandparents George, Kimiko, and Rosaria.

La lontananza spegne i fuochi piccoli ma accende quelli grandi. Dedicato ai nonni George, Kmiko, e Rosaria.

A distância extingue os pequenos fogos, mas levanta as maiores. Dedicado ao nosso avós George, Kimiko, e Rosaria.

www.rhythmntyping.com

ALL OF THE INSTRUCTIONS WRITTEN IN THIS BOOK CAN BE HEARD IN ITS ENTIRETY ON THE AUDIO INSTRUCTIONS-PAGE OF THIS BOOK`S WEBSITE.

Visit this book`s website at:

www.rhythmntyping.com

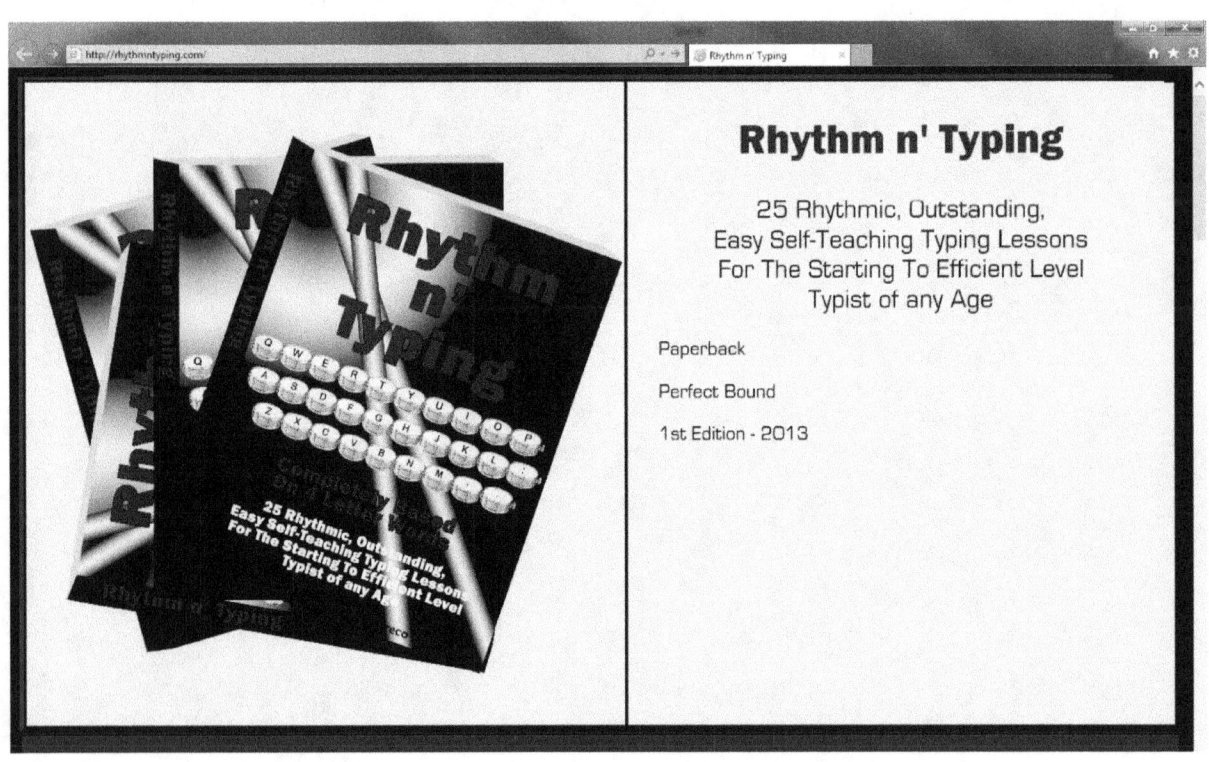

Contents

Part One

Presentation	1
Concept	2
4 Letter Model	3
Typing Endurance	4
Your Setting at the Typing Station	5
The Typing Posture	7
The Eye-line	8
The Keyboard	10
Fingering	11
Tips for Good Typing	12
Monitor View and Document Setup	14
OUR RHYTHMIC TYPING SYSTEM	16
PATTERN OF THE 7 EXERCISES	17
Reminder of General Rules for Good Typing Practice	19
Home Row	22
Top Row	27
Bottom Row	32
Number Row	36
1st Lesson	39
2nd Lesson	43
3rd Lesson	47
4th Lesson	51
5th Lesson	55
6th Lesson	59
7th Lesson	63
8th Lesson	67
9th Lesson	71
10th Lesson	75
11th Lesson	79

12th Lesson	83
13th Lesson	87
14th Lesson	91
15th Lesson	95
16th Lesson	99
17th Lesson	103
18th Lesson	107
19th Lesson	111
20th Lesson	115
21st Lesson	119
22nd Lesson	123
23rd Lesson	127
24th Lesson	131
25th Lesson	135
Advanced Practice on all the Words in the 25 Lessons	139
Practice on Sentences	144
Practice on Paragraphs	148
Other Signs and Symbols	149
Exclamation Point	150
At	151
Number or Pound	152
Dollar	153
Percent	154
Ampersand	155
Asterisk or Star	156
Parenthesis	157
Hyphen - Dash - Minus	158
Underscore	160
Equal	161
Plus	162
Letter Samples	163
Regular 1.0 line spacing	164
Changed line spacing	165
Bolded text	166

  Indented text 167
  Italicized text 168
  Justified text 169
  Numbered list 170
  Bulleted list 171
  Bordered text 172
  Underlined text 173
Table of Roman Numerals 174
Frequently Asked Questions 176
About This Book 176
 LITTLE DICTIONARY 178

Part One

Presentation

Rhythm n' Typing, it goes without say that rhythm is the driving element of this typing book, actually almost all its practice contents are based on rhythm. Rhythm is what makes this book a very effective media of teaching typing; and rhythm is also what makes the task of learning typing a much more enjoyable experience.

Part One of this book includes: its technical presentation; exercises on the three rows of letters on the keyboard; exercises on the numbers; and most of all the charts with the explanation of our rhythmic typing system

Part Two contains the 25 progressive typing lessons each made-up of the technical developments of a group of 3 basic rhyming words of 4 letters.

Part Three is made of: typing practice on sentences under the form of proverbs whose words never exceed four letters; more advanced practice on the content and format of a variety of actual mail that we all receive or send; and the Little Dictionary.

The contents of **Rhythm n' Typing** are presented in a brief and well structured way with the purpose of being clear to the eyes of the student. That is the reason why most of the written instructions are concentrated in the early pages of this book, leaving the pages containing the actual exercises free of any visually interfering or distractive writings.

Concept

The concept of **Rhythm n' Typing** is mostly based on groups of three rhyming words of 4 letters each, letters that are to be systematically practiced 1 per second, 2 per second, 3 per second, 4 per second and the combinations of the above. Ultimately, each and every word in the lessons is to be typed rhythmically one per second. Rhythm in this book is the dominant element.

In this innovating, advanced, modern typing book you will immediately start practicing on real, complete words, rather than go through months of practicing just on plain letters and signs like with most traditional typing books.

This concept, obviously, is not a casual one but rather the result of a series of time consuming tests at the keyboard by the authors, which in many instances relied on feedback from beginner typing students about the way they would like a typing book to be structured in order for them to enjoy learning from it.

After several different practical tests in the search for the ultimate typing guide for beginner typists, finally the authors convened and consolidated **Rhythm n' Typing**.

4 Letter Model

The 4 Letter Word Model used in this book was established after counting several large samples of words taken randomly from the pages of a variety of books and magazines, then examining the statistical data collected. From this research the authors have found that on average about 55% to 65% of the words of any printed text are made up of 4 letter words or less.

Accordingly, to alleviate the beginner typist from the burden of practicing on text sources loaded with long, complicated words, the authors of this book have come-up with the 4 Letter Word Model, a simple system yet a smart and effective one. This model undoubtedly simplifies, for the beginner, the task involving the visual individuation of the location of each letter and sign on the keys of the keyboard. The reasoning is that short words also employ the frequent use of the space-bar, and a stroke of space-bar is a precious, convenient second in which to quickly regroup your concentration and reflexes, allowing time for your eyes to visually locate the next four letters on the keyboard and for your fingers to comfortably strike the four corresponding keys.

Typing Endurance

Typing Endurance at the keyboard is the gradual adapting process of the body and the mind to overcome the fatigue generated by the task of typing for hours at a time.

The authors of this book, as a means for reassurance, want you to know up-front that for the first few weeks of your typing practice, you will probably be able to endure this task for at most twenty minutes at a time; thereafter your patience would easily run out, if so, don't be concerned, that is the normal reaction expected from a beginner typist. Endurance at the keyboard will come with time, practice, necessity and love for this task.

Accordingly, the authors conveniently arranged the timing practice of each lesson in this book to be within twenty minutes range. With time, the best way for you to start raising the bar of your endurance at the keyboard would be to practice the same lesson two or three times in the same session. Subsequently, you can further raise your endurance bar by typing down any interesting articles published in magazines or newspapers regarding any of your favorite subjects. Another useful great way to solidify your endurance is by neatly typing down your school's written assignments or by typing down the exact text of any letter you receive in your mailbox.

Endurance should be undoubtedly one of the main goals of the typist beside speed and spelling accuracy.

Your Setting at the Typing Station

- Free your workstation from any extra, loose, unorganized, distractive objects such as pens, pencils, erasers, notebooks, books, paper, etc.

- When using a standard keyboard, you can easily create an inclination by lifting the legs beneath it; however, if you are using a laptop on a table, do not just lay it flat, but rather use a laptop-stand to create the correct inclination which will ease the flexing of your fingers and wrists throughout all the typing they will be doing. Another benefit for using a laptop-stand is that it elevates the laptop from the table creating airflow beneath it and reducing heat buildup in the laptop's components preventing them from overheating. (See figure 1)

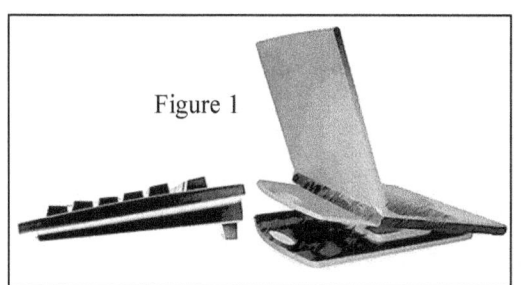

Figure 1

- For easy, comfortable reading-clarity, it is important to have good lighting illuminating the pages of this book or any other text on the stand, for this, a desk or floor gooseneck lamp pointed directly on the pages of the book will perfectly suit your needs. Avoid getting direct light in your eyes.

- When getting set for practice, place and adjust the stand with this book on it at a comfortable height in relation to your eyes, such that you don't have to bend your neck or back downward or upward in order to read from it. The best position to set this book, or any other text, is to place it on a desk stand on the left or right side of the monitor at an angle slightly slanted under the light of a gooseneck lamp. If on your worktable there is no room for a book rest or a lamp, simply use a music stand or something similar for your reading source and a floor lamp for lighting and you will be comfortably set. (See figure 2)

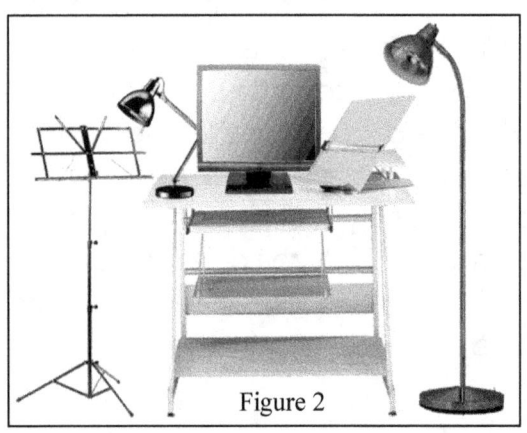
Figure 2

- When using a stand, you may sometimes need to fasten your text sources, the ones that are difficult to keep standing straight or fully open on it, such as a single soft sheet of paper, a newspaper page, a thick bulky book, an oversized brochure and so on. To prevent these from flying-away, folding-over, falling-off, or closing-up from the stand, you can use a variety of convenient little household gadgets such as paper clips, bag clips, elastic bands and other things of this nature. These handy gadgets are helpful in securing the texts sources on to the stand and keeping the page(s) of the text source(s) flat, avoiding annoying creases, bumps, crumples, or glare on the page making it much easier to read from. (See figure 3)

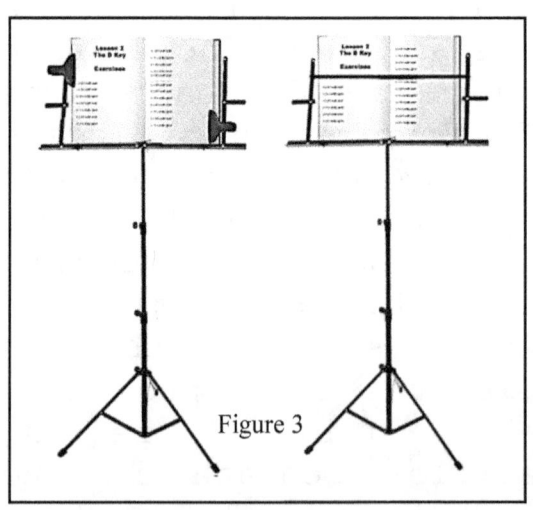
Figure 3

The Typing Posture

Figure 4

- When sitting down at the workstation preparing for your daily typing practice, check that your posture is correct; for the correct typing posture refer to figure 4 above.

- For maximum, long-lasting sitting comfort, make sure that your back is upright and by any means pressed against the backrest of the chair.

- Be seated at a comfortable height and distance from the keyboard (see figure 4 on page 7).

- Use the same type of low-back or mid-back chair (see figure 4 on page 7 and figure 5 on page 8).

- Adjust the height of the seat so your upper arms hang by your side with your elbows bent at 90° (see figure 4 on page 7).

- Adjust the backrest of your chair to give support to your lower back.

- Hold out your wrists in a straight neutral position not bent upward or downward.

- Keep your feet flat on the ground; utilize a footrest to place your feet if necessary.

The Eye-line

The Comfortable Eye-Line to Retain on the Monitor while Typing

Figure 5

- Adjust the monitor so that your eyes are aligned with the top part of the screen (see figure 5).

- Position the monitor about 2 feet away from your eyes.

- Use a stand next to the monitor to hold your text sources upright rather than laying them flat on the surface of the table you are using.

While typing, for the comfort of your neck, back, and eyes, keep the ongoing typing line within the upper part of the screen. This can be achieved by periodically moving the already typed lines upward, you will manage to do so using the mouse, either by rolling its wheel or by using its pointer to move the scroll bar on the right side of the window you are working with.

The Eye-Line comfort height also applies to the text on the stand which you are reading and typing from. The text has to be at the same height as the screen, placed on a tabletop stand or a floor stand on the left or right side of the monitor. One way to have a truly mobile and efficient stand is to use a music stand which can easily be raised or lowered and moved to either side of the table or computer station at your convenience.

The correct height of the Eye-Line in typing directly correlates with the upright comfort position of your neck and back, which is ultimately a determinant factor for a long and comfortable session of typing.

The Keyboard

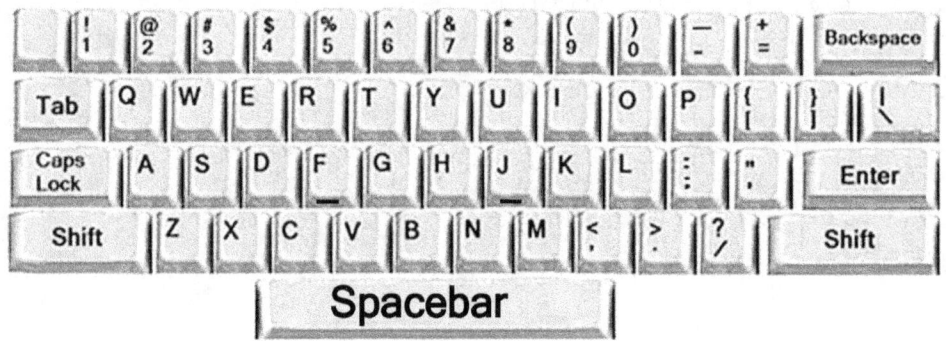

Figure 6

Tab — to indent a word

Caps Lock — to make a letter UPPERCASE

Backspace — to delete any previous letter, sign or number

Enter — to start new paragraphs and for vertical spacing

Shift — to type the alternate upper characters on a key

Spacebar — to space-out words, signs and numbers

Fingering

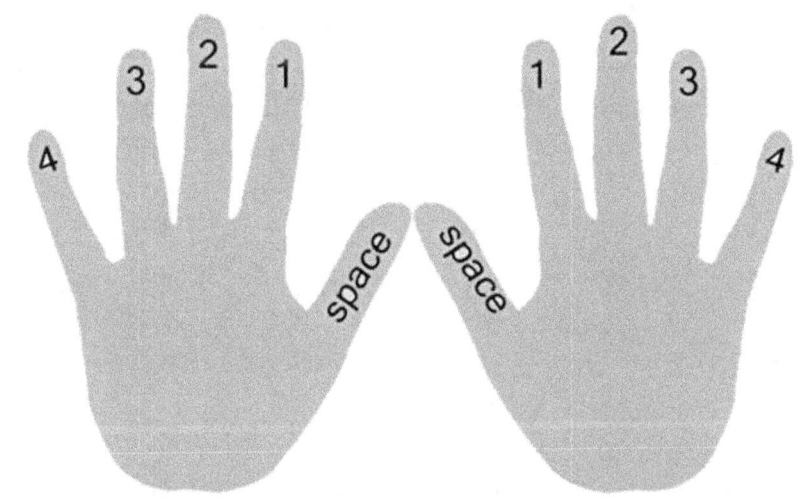

Figure 7

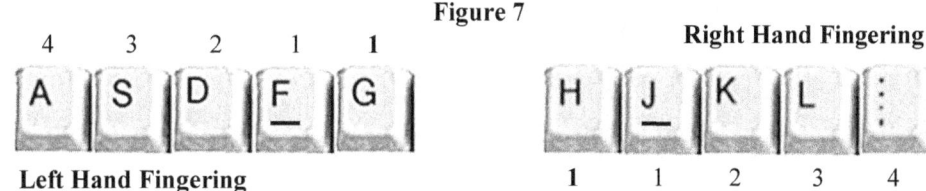

Left Hand Fingering

Right Hand Fingering

The little numbers above the letters, the signs, and the numbers, indicate the fingering for the keys to be punched with the fingers of the left hand.

The little numbers below the letters, the signs, and the numbers, indicate the fingering for the keys to be punched with the fingers of the right hand.

The bold **1** above or below a letter, sign, or number indicates an extension of the left or right hand first finger.

Most Left handed typists usually space with the left thumb.

Most Right handed typists usually space with the right thumb.

Thumbs are only used to type the space bar.

Tips for Good Typing

- In the beginning, practice the exercises in this book looking back and forth at the words in the text of a lesson and the position of your fingers on the keys. After, with time and practice you will be able to acquire *Touch-Typing* skills, the technique in which your eyes are mostly looking at the text that has been typed and rarely down at your fingers on the keyboard.

- When typing, keep the finger tips of both hands in constant contact with the keys: do not retreat the momentarily unused hand from the keyboard. The constant positions of the resting fingers are always on the Home Row. In order to keep your hands in the correct position on the keyboard make sure that the tip of the first finger of the left hand touches the bump on the F key and the tip of the first finger of the right hand touches the bump on the J key. From the Home Row extend your fingers to the lower or upper rows to type other letters and then return your fingers to the Home Row.
The thumbs are always positioned on the space bar.

- It would be a very good practice technique to speak-out the words before typing them and each letter of those words at the moment that you are typing them, such a task will add more solidity to your skills.

- When you are finished typing the words of a lesson, clear the screen by deleting all the words from that lesson. By doing so, you will always have a blank document which will give you a clear vision of what you are going to type next.

- For the first few weeks, practice the exercises making sure that your fingers tap on the keys vigorously. You'll need to gain strength in your fingers first; softness, agility and speed will follow later with time and practice.

- For maximum typing efficiency, make sure that when you start practicing, your hands are warm and elastic, if not that can be easily achieved by washing your hands with warm water and soap; also, when your hands are dry soften them by applying lotion.

- While typing, keep your wrists lifted from the table so that your finger articulation and speed can function at its best and to avoid strain and stiffness in your hands and wrists (see figure A and B).

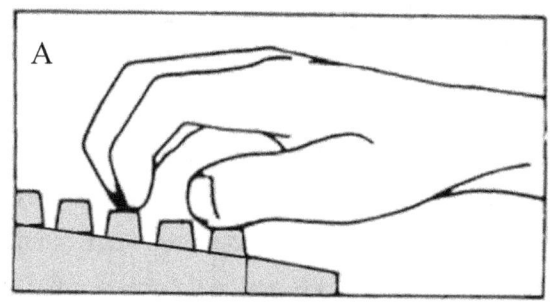

correct wrist position

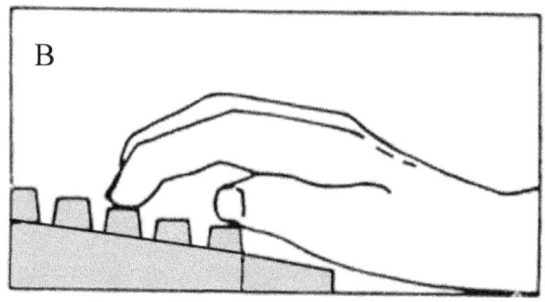

incorrect wrist position

Monitor View and Document Setup

Book View	Monitor View
¹ ⁴ f a l l ₃ ₃ ff aa ll ll fff aaa lll lll ffff aaaa llll llll f ff a aa l ll l ll f fff a aaa l lll l lll f ffff a aaaa l llll l llll *This is the way that the exercises appear on the pages of this book.*	F a l l Ff aa ll ll Fff aaa lll lll Ffff aaaa llll llll F ff a aa l ll l ll F fff a aaa l lll l lll F ffff a aaaa l llll l llll *This is the way the words of the exercises will appear on your screen after you have typed them.*

Note, The student will type all of the letters and words always in **size 20 Microsoft San Serif font.**

After getting settled at your typing station, before practicing the exercises in this book, you must first setup your Word document to **Print Layout view** so you can get that particular old fashioned feeling that you are typing a page on an actual traditional typewriter.

To setup your Word document in Print Layout view, first click on View in the toolbar then click on Print Layout view.

In order to have a good view of the text that you are typing, adjust the font size based on your screen resolution; for your best eyesight comfort the authors suggest a font **size of 20**.

To adjust the font size, first click on the font size list in the font group on the home tab then click on size 20.

To get a good, clear view of the letters and words you are typing on the monitor it is important that you keep the line that you are typing well spaced; the authors suggest to set the line spacing at **1.5**. To achieve that nicely spaced clear view, first click on Line Spacing in the Paragraph group on the home tab then click on 1.5.

After completely typing each pattern of exercises, tap on the **Enter key** to start a new line so that your next line of typing can be displayed clearly just the way it appears on the pages of the book (*see monitor view on page 14*).

Do* *not type the exercises of a lesson in one long dragging line.

OUR RHYTHMIC TYPING SYSTEM

a	UNIT SIZE LETTERS	= TYPE 1 LETTER PER SECOND
aa	DOUBLET SIZE LETTERS	= TYPE 2 LETTERS PER SECOND
aaa	TRIPLET SIZE LETTERS	= TYPE 3 LETTERS PER SECOND
aaaa	QUADRUPLET SIZE LETTERS	= TYPE 4 LETTERS PER SECOND
▭	1 SPACE	= TYPE 1 SPACE PER SECOND *ALWAYS*

a b c d = letter *space* letter *space* letter *space* letter *space*
(4 letters + 4 spaces = 8 seconds)

aa bb cc dd = 2 letters *space* 2 letters *space* 2 letters *space* 2 letters *space*
(8 letters + 4 spaces = 8 seconds)

aaa bbb ccc ddd = 3 letters *space* 3 letters *space* 3 letters *space* 3 letters *space*
(12 letters + 4 spaces = 8 seconds)

aaaa bbbb cccc dddd = 4 letters *space* 4 letters *space* 4 letters *space* 4 letters *space*
(16 letters + 4 spaces = 8 seconds)

abcd = letter letter letter letter *space*
(4 letters + 1 space = 5 seconds)

PATTERN OF THE 7 EXERCISES

I	1 Second **a** □ Space 1 Second	1 Second **b** □ Space 1 Second	1 Second **c** □ Space 1 Second	1 Second **d** □ Space 1 Second
II	1 Second **aa** □ Space 1 Second	1 Second **bb** □ Space 1 Second	1 Second **cc** □ Space 1 Second	1 Second **dd** □ Space 1 Second
III	1 Second **aaa** □ Space 1 Second	1 Second **bbb** □ Space 1 Second	1 Second **ccc** □ Space 1 Second	1 Second **ddd** □ Space 1 Second
IV	1 Second **aaaa** □ Space 1 Second	1 Second **bbbb** □ Space 1 Second	1 Second **cccc** □ Space 1 Second	1 Second **dddd** □ Space 1 Second

	1 Second		1 Second		1 Second		1 Second	
V	a	☐ Space 1 Second	aa	☐ Space 1 Second	b	☐ Space 1 Second	bb	☐ Space 1 Second
VI	a	☐ Space 1 Second	aaa	☐ Space 1 Second	b	☐ Space 1 Second	bbb	☐ Space 1 Second
VII	a	☐ Space 1 Second	aaaa	☐ Space 1 Second	b	☐ Space 1 Second	bbbb	☐ Space 1 Second

The exercise patterns I, II, III, IV, V, VI, VII are always the same throughout the book.

Reminder of General Rules for Good Typing Practice

To have a clear view of your typing it would be best to set your line spacing at **1.5,** to get such a setting first click on *Line Spacing* in the *Paragraph group* on the *home tab* then click on **1.5.**
Hit the **Enter** key after each line of words.

♦

Type the exercises in **lowercase Microsoft San Serif** *font size* **20** on a page set-up in **print layout view.**

♦

The numbers **above** the letters indicate the use of the fingers of the **left hand.**
The numbers **below** the letters indicate the use of the fingers of the **right hand.**
Bold **1**'s indicate the extension of the **1st finger** (do not type the fingering numbers).

The **constant positions** of the resting fingers are always on the *Home Row*. The tip of the first finger of the left hand touches the <u>**bump**</u> on the **F** key and the tip of the first finger of the right hand touches the <u>**bump**</u> on the **J** key. From the *Home Row* extend your fingers to the lower or upper rows to type other letters and then return your fingers to the Home Row. *The thumbs are always positioned on the space bar.*

◆

Re-type each pattern a **few times** around.

◆

After typing the exercises of an entire lesson, **delete** all the words from the screen for your next round of typing practice.

◆

All the patterns in the exercises have to be typed with rhythm, as explained in the scheme on pages 17 - 18.

Home Row

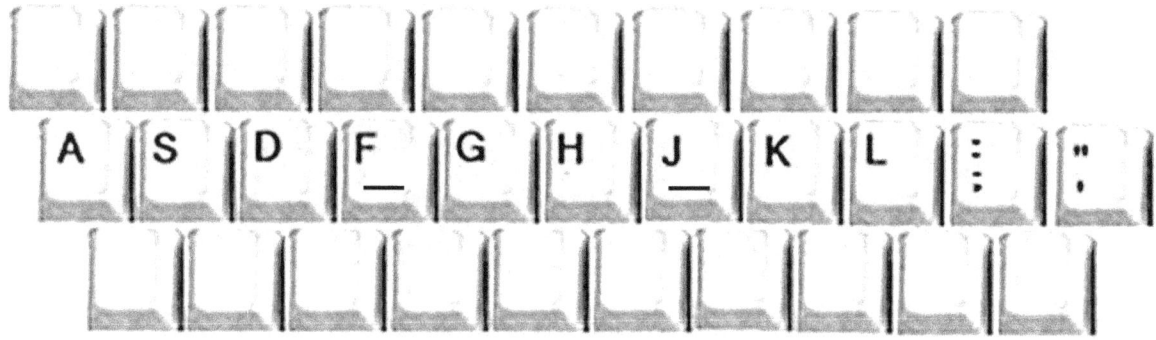

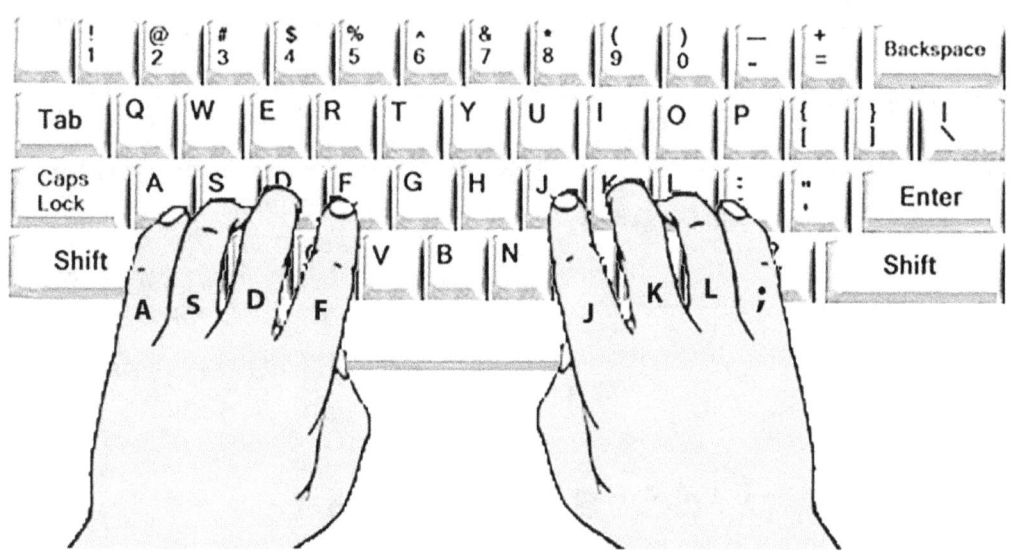

Home Row

Left hand fingering
4   3   2   1   **1**

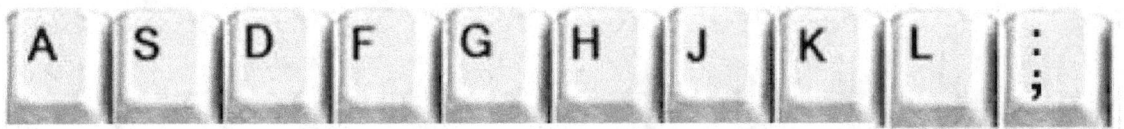

                      1   1   2   3   4
Right hand fingering

Home Row : Left Hand

Exercises

Reminders

The little numbers above and below the letters indicate the fingering, **do not type them**.

Type the letters **all the same size** using font size 20.

For complete rhythm outline see chart on **pages 17-18**, or listen to the rhythm on the Audio Instructions section of this book's **website** .

Always keep steady rhytm.

          1   2   3   4
I)   f   d   s   a

II)   ff   dd   ss   aa

III)   fff   ddd   sss   aaa

IV)   ffff   dddd   ssss   aaaa

V)   f ff   d dd   s ss   a aa

VI)   f fff   d ddd   s sss   a aaa

VII)   f ffff   d dddd   s ssss   a aaaa

Home Row : Right Hand

Exercises

I)   **j k l ;**
           1 2 3 4

II)   **jj kk ll** ;;

III)   **jjj kkk lll** ;;;

IV)   jjjj kkkk llll ;;;;

V)   **j jj k kk l ll ; ;;**

VI)   **j** jjj **k** kkk **l** lll **;** ;;;

VII)   **j** jjjj **k** kkkk **l** llll **;** ;;;;

Home Row : Left & Right Hand

Exercises

I)   1   2   3   4
     f j d k s l a ;
     1   2   3   4

II)   **ff   jj   dd   kk   ss   ll   aa   ;;**

III)   **fff   jjj   ddd   kkk   sss   lll   aaa   ;;;**

IV)   ffff   jjjj   dddd   kkkk   ssss   llll   aaaa   ;;;;

V)   **f** ff **j** jj **d** dd **k** kk **s** ss **l** ll
    a aa **;** ;;

VI)   **f** fff **j** jjj **d** ddd **k** kkk **s** sss **l** lll
     a aaa **;** ;;;

VII)   **f** ffff **j** jjjj **d** dddd **k** kkkk **s** ssss **l** llll
     a aaaa **;** ;;;;

Home Row : Left Hand & Right Hand
1ST Finger the FG - JH Extensions

Exercises

I)   ¹ ¹
     f g j h
        ₁ ₁

II)   **ff gg jj hh**

III)   **fff ggg jjj hhh**

IV)   ffff gggg jjjj hhhh

V)   **f** ff **g** gg **j** jj **h** hh

VI)   **f** fff **g** ggg **j** jjj **h** hhh

VII)   **f** ffff **g** gggg **j** jjjj **h** hhhh

Top Row

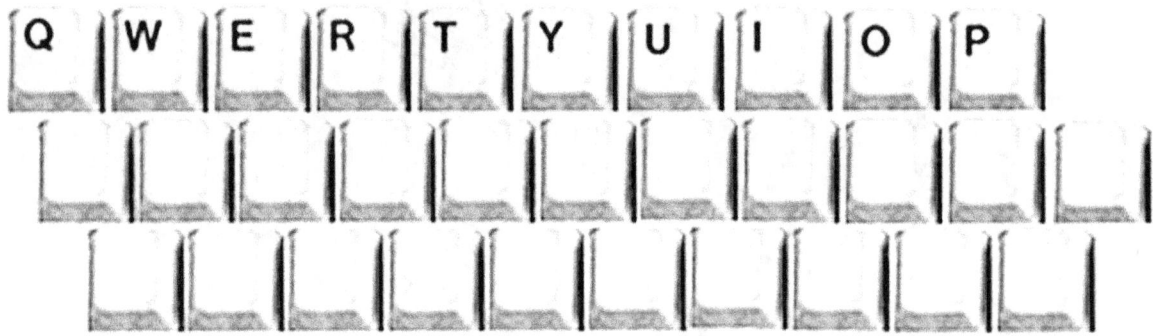

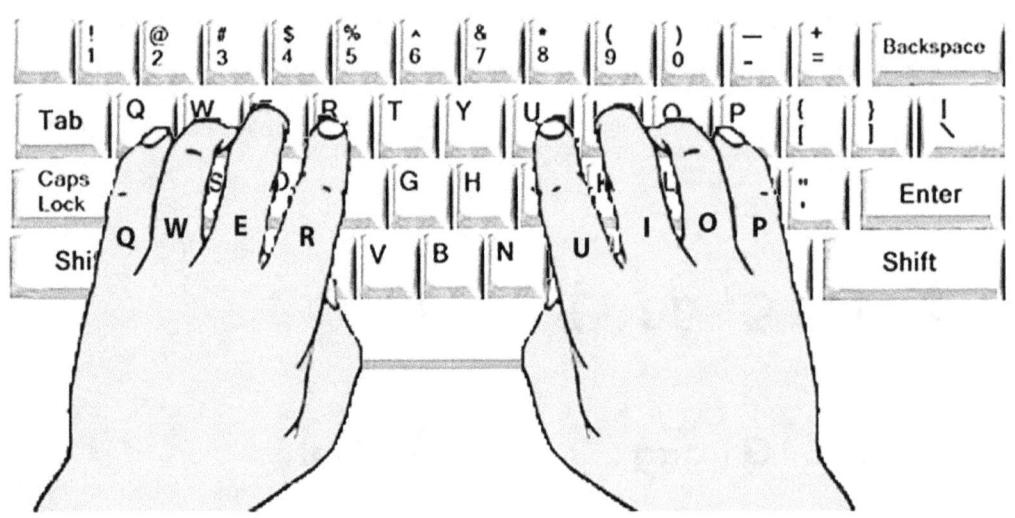

Top Row

Left hand fingering
4 3 2 1 **1**

Q W E R T Y U I O P

1 1 2 3 4
Right hand fingering

Top Row : Left Hand

Exercises

Reminders

*The little numbers above and below the letters indicate the fingering, **do not type them**.*

*Type the letters **all the same size** using font size 20.*

*For complete rhythm outline see chart on **pages 17-18**, or listen to the rhythm on the Audio Instructions section of this book's **website** .*

Always keep steady rhytm.

I)
    1 2 3 4
r e w q

II) **rr ee ww qq**

III) **rrr eee www qqq**

IV) **rrrr eeee wwww qqqq**

V) **r** rr **e** ee **w** ww **q** qq

VI) **r** rrr **e** eee **w** www **q** qqq

VII) **r** rrrr **e** eeee **w** wwww **q** qqqq

Top Row : Right Hand

Exercises

I) **u i o p**
    1   2   3   4

II) **uu ii oo pp**

III) **uuu iii ooo ppp**

IV) uuuu iiii oooo pppp

V) **u** uu **i** ii **o** oo **p** pp

VI) **u** uuu **i** iii **o** ooo **p** ppp

VII) **u** uuuu **i** iiii **o** oooo **p** pppp

Top Row : Left & Right Hand

Exercises

I)   1   2   3   4

       r u e i w o q p

       1   2   3   4

II)   **rr uu ee ii ww oo qq pp**

III) **rrr uuu eee iii www ooo qqq ppp**

IV) rrrr uuuu eeee iiii wwww oooo qqqq pppp

V)   **r** rr **u** uu **e** ee **i** ii **w** ww **o** oo
      q qq **p** pp

VI) **r** rrr **u** uuu **e** eee **i** iii **w** www **o** ooo
      q qqq **p** ppp

VII) **r** rrrr **u** uuuu **e** eeee **i** iiii **w** wwww **o** oooo
      q qqqq **p** pppp

Top Row : Left Hand & Right Hand
1ST Finger the RT - UY Extensions

Exercises

I)   1   **1**
     r t u y
         1   **1**

II)   **rr tt uu yy**

III)   **rrr ttt uuu yyy**

IV)   rrrr tttt uuuu yyyy

V)   **r rr t tt u uu y yy**

VI)   **r** rrr **t** ttt **u** uuu **y** yyy

VII)   **r** rrrr **t** tttt **u** uuuu **y** yyyy

Bottom Row

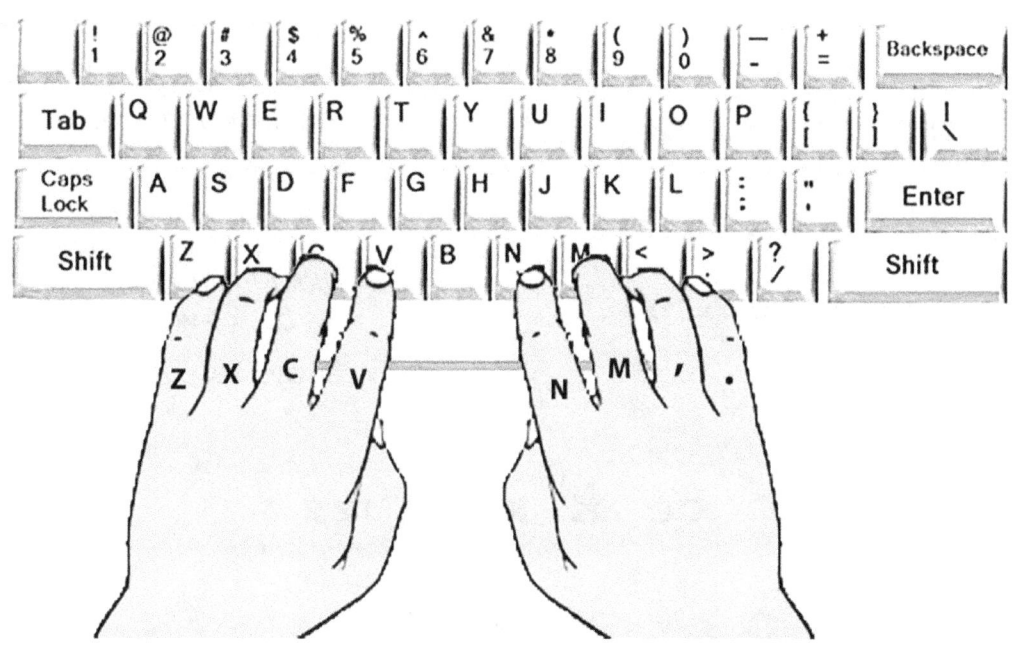

31

Bottom Row

Left hand fingering
4   3   2   1   **1**

1   2   3   4
Right hand fingering

Bottom Row : Left Hand

Exercises

Reminders

The little numbers above and below the letters indicate the fingering, **do not type them**.

Type the letters **all the same size** using font size 20.

For complete rhythm outline see chart on **pages 17-18**, or listen to the rhythm on the Audio Instructions section of this book's **website** .

Always keep steady rhytm.

I)   1   2   3   4
     V   C   X   Z

II)   **vv   cc   xx   zz**

III)   **vvv   ccc   xxx   zzz**

IV)   **vvvv   cccc   xxxx   zzzz**

V)   **V vv C cc X xx Z zz**

VI)   **V vvv C ccc X xxx Z zzz**

VII)   **V vvvv C cccc X xxxx Z zzzz**

Bottom Row : Right Hand

Exercises

I) **n m** , .
    1 2 3 4

II) **nn mm** ,, ..

III) **nnn mmm** ,,, ...

IV) **nnnn mmmm** ,,,, ...

V) **n** nn **m** mm , ,, . ..

VI) **n** nnn **m** mmm , ,,, ...

VII) **n** nnnn **m** mmmm , ,,,, ...

Bottom Row : Left & Right Hand

Exercises

I)
    1   2   3   4
v n c m x , z .
    1   2   3   4

II) **vv nn cc mm xx ,, zz ..**

III) **vvv nnn ccc mmm xxx ,,, zzz ...**

IV) **vvvv nnnn cccc mmmm xxxx ,,,, zzzz ....**

V) **v** vv **n** nn **c** cc **m** mm **x** xx **,** ,, **z** zz **.** ..

VI) **v** vvv **n** nnn **c** ccc **m** mmm **x** xxx **,** ,,, **z** zzz **.** ...

VII) **v** vvvv **n** nnnn **c** cccc **m** mmmm **x** xxxx **,** ,,,, **z** zzzz **.** ....

Bottom Row : Left Hand
1ˢᵀ Finger the VB Extension

Exercises

I)   1 **1**
    v b

II)   **vv bb**

III) **vvv bbb**

IV) **vvvv bbbb**

V)   **v** vv **b** bb

VI) **v** vvv **b** bbb

VII) **v** vvvv **b** bbbb

Note:
Bottom Row right hand does not have a 1ˢᵗ finger extension

Number Row

Number Row : Left Hand

Exercises

Reminders

The little numbers above and below the letters indicate the fingering, **do not type them**.

Type the letters **all the same size** using font size 20.

For complete rhythm outline see chart on **pages 17-18**, or listen to the rhythm on the Audio Instructions section of this book's **website** .

Always keep steady rhytm.

I) **1 2 3 4 5**

II) **11 22 33 44 55**

III) 111 222 333 444 555

IV) 1111 2222 3333 4444 5555

V) **1** 11 **2** 22 **3** 33 **4** 44 **5** 55

VI) **1** 111 **2** 222 **3** 333 **4** 444 **5** 555

VII) **1** 1111 **2** 2222 **3** 3333 **4** 4444 **5** 5555

Number Row : Right Hand

Exercises

I)   **0 9 8 7 6**

II)   **00 99 88 77 66**

III)   **000 999 888 777 666**

IV)   0000 9999 8888 7777 6666

V)   **0** 00 **9** 99 **8** 88 **7** 77 **6** 66

VI)   **0** 000 **9** 999 **8** 888 **7** 777 **6** 666

VII)   **0** 0000 **9** 9999 **8** 8888 **7** 7777 **6** 6666

Part Two

1ˢᵗ Lesson

FALL • **G**ALL • **H**ALL

Exercises

I)   ¹f ⁴a l l
           ₃ ₃

II)   ff aa ll ll

III) fff aaa lll lll

IV) ffff aaaa llll llll

V)   f ff a aa l ll l ll

VI) f fff a aaa l lll l lll

VII) f ffff a aaaa l llll l llll

> **Reminders**
>
> The little numbers above and below the letters indicate the fingering, **do not type them**.
>
> Type the letters **all the same size** using font size 20.
>
> For complete rhythm outline see chart on **pages 17-18**, or listen to the rhythm on the Audio Instructions section of this book's **website**.
>
> Always keep steady rhytm.

I)   **1**   4
     g a l l
        3   3

II) gg aa ll ll

III) ggg aaa lll lll

IV) gggg aaaa llll llll

V) g gg a aa l ll l ll

VI) g ggg a aaa l lll l lll

VII) g gggg a aaaa l llll l llll

                1   4
I)   h a l l
              3 3

II)   hh aa ll ll

III)   hhh aaa lll lll

IV)   hhhh aaaa llll llll

V)   h hh a aa l ll l ll

VI)   h hhh a aaa l lll l lll

VII)   h hhhh a aaaa l llll l llll

Type words and spaces one key per second

Exercise

fall gall hall gall hall fall hall fall gall

THE USE OF THE SEMICOLON AND COLON

Semicolon   ;

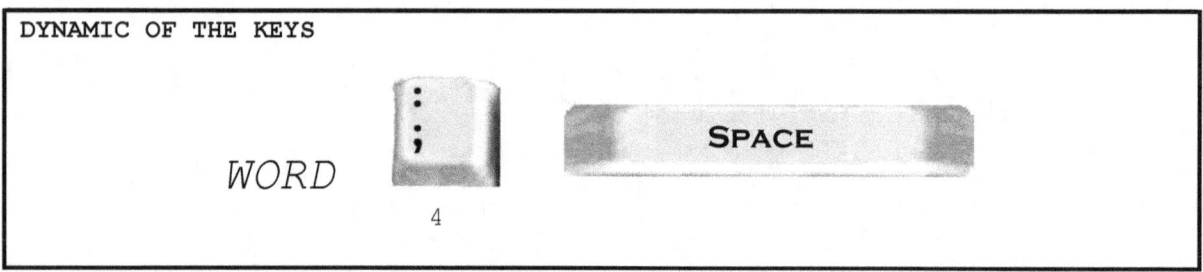

Type words, signs and spaces one key per second

Exercise

fall; gall; hall;

Colon   :

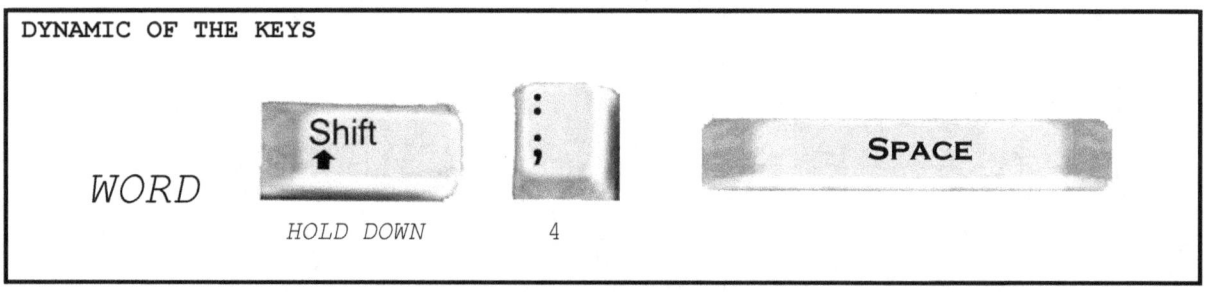

Type words, signs and spaces one key per second

Exercise

fall: gall: gall:

2nd Lesson

FL**AG** • DR**AG** • SH**AG**

Exercises

I)   ¹f   ⁴l   **¹**a   g
               ₃

Reminders

*The little numbers above and below the letters indicate the fingering, **do not type them**.*

*Type the letters **all the same size** using font size 20.*

*For complete rhythm outline see chart on **pages 17-18**, or listen to the rhythm on the Audio Instructions section of this book's **website** .*

Always keep steady rhytm.

II)   ff   ll   aa   gg

III)   fff   lll   aaa   ggg

IV)   ffff   llll   aaaa   gggg

V)   f   ff   l   ll   a   aa   g   gg

VI)   f   fff   l   lll   a   aaa   g   ggg

VII)   f   ffff   l   llll   a   aaaa   g   gggg

```
        2  1  4  1
I )    d  r  a  g


II )   dd  rr  aa  gg


III )  ddd  rrr  aaa  ggg


IV )   dddd  rrrr  aaaa  gggg


V )    d  dd   r  rr   a  aa   g  gg


VI )   d  ddd   r  rrr   a  aaa   g  ggg


VII )  d  dddd   r  rrrr   a  aaaa   g  gggg
```

I)   ³   ⁴ **1**
    s h a g
      1

II) ss hh aa gg

III) sss hhh aaa ggg

IV) ssss hhhh aaaa gggg

V)   s ss h hh a aa g gg

VI) s sss h hhh a aaa g ggg

VII) s ssss h hhhh a aaaa g gggg

Type and spaces the three words normally

Exercise

flag drag shag drag shag flag shag flag drag

45

THE USE OF THE SEMICOLON AND COLON

Semicolon   ;

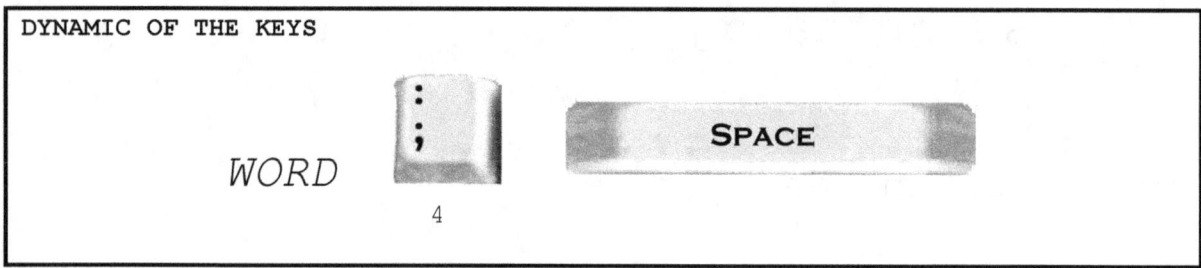

Exercise

flag; drag; shag;

Colon   :

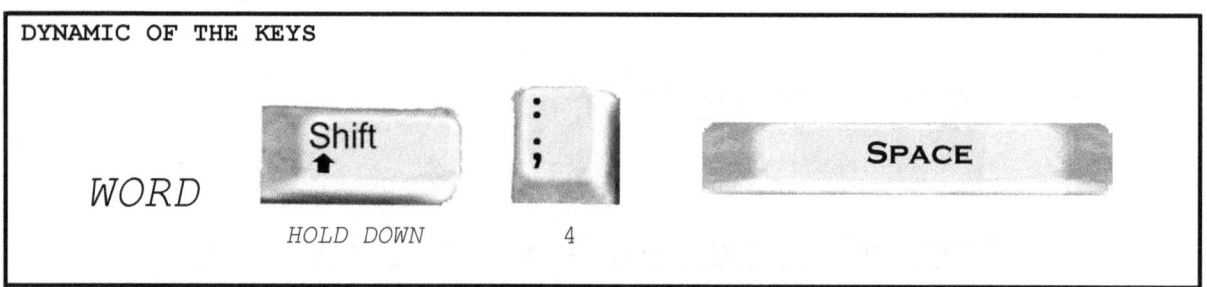

Exercise

flag: drag: shag:

3rd Lesson

FLEE • *GLEE* • *FREE*

Exercises

```
         1   2 2
I)      f l e e
          3
```

II)   ff ll ee ee

III)   fff lll eee eee

IV)   ffff llll eeee eeee

Reminders

*The little numbers above and below the letters indicate the fingering, **do not type them**.*

*Type the letters **all the same size** using font size 20.*

*For complete rhythm outline see chart on **pages 17-18**, or listen to the rhythm on the Audio Instructions section of this book's **website**.*

Always keep steady rhytm.

V)   f ff l ll e ee e ee

VI)   f fff l lll e eee e eee

VII)   f ffff l llll e eeee e eeee

47

          1   2   2
I)   g l e e
            3

II)   gg ll ee ee

III)   ggg lll eee eee

IV)   gggg llll eeee eeee

V)   g gg l ll e ee e ee

VI)   g ggg l lll e eee e eee

VII)   g gggg l llll e eeee e eeee

　　　　　　1　1　2　2
I)　　　f　r　e　e

II)　　ff rr ee ee

III)　 fff rrr eee eee

IV)　 ffff rrrr eeee eeee

V)　 f ff r rr e ee e ee

VI)　 f fff r rrr e eee e eee

VII)　f ffff r rrrr e eeee e eeee

Type and space the three words normally

Exercise

flee glee free glee free flee free flee glee

THE USE OF THE SEMICOLON AND COLON

Semicolon   ;

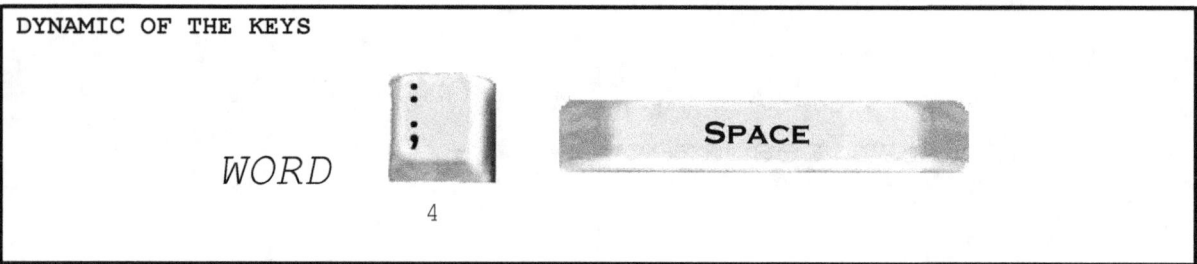

Exercise

flee; glee; free;

Colon   :

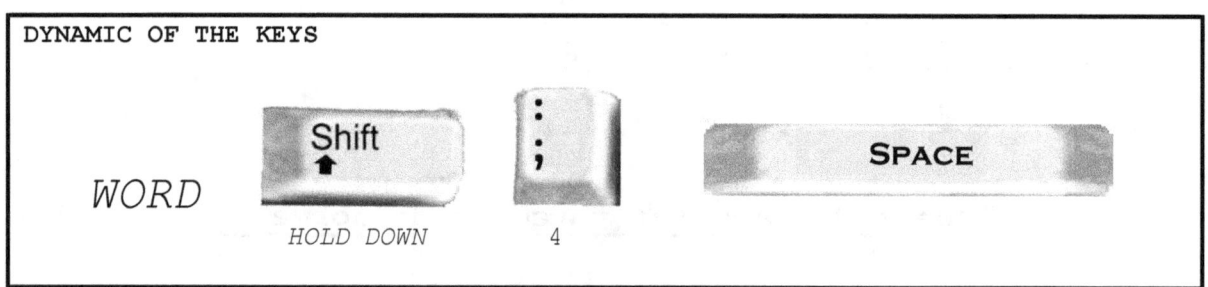

Exercise

flee: glee: free:

4th Lesson

FOIL • SOIL • TOIL

Exercises

I) f o i l
    (1 above l; 3 2 3 below f o l)

II) ff oo ii ll

III) fff ooo iii lll

IV) ffff oooo iiii llll

> **Reminders**
>
> The little numbers above and below the letters indicate the fingering, **do not type them**.
>
> Type the letters **all the same size** using font size 20.
>
> For complete rhythm outline see chart on **pages 17-18**, or listen to the rhythm on the Audio Instructions section of this book's **website**.
>
> Always keep steady rhytm.

V) f ff o oo i ii l ll

VI) f fff o ooo i iii l lll

VII) f ffff o oooo i iiii l llll

I)

$\overset{3}{s}\ \underset{3}{o}\ \underset{2}{i}\ \underset{3}{l}$

II)

ss oo ii ll

III)

sss ooo iii lll

IV)

ssss oooo iiii llll

V)

S ss O oo i ii l ll

VI)

S sss O ooo i iii l lll

VII)

S ssss O oooo i iiii l llll

I) t o i l
        3 2 3
     1

II) tt oo ii ll

III) ttt ooo iii lll

IV) tttt oooo iiii llll

V) t tt o oo i ii l ll

VI) t ttt o ooo i iii l lll

VII) t tttt o oooo i iiii l llll

Type and space the three words normally

Exercise

foil soil toil soil toil foil toil foil soil

THE USE OF THE APOSTROPHE AND QUOTATION MARKS

*These two punctuation signs are both located within the same key in the home row just to the right of the semicolon and colon key. To use the **apostrophe**, just punch that key with the 4th finger of your right hand. To use the **quotation marks** (both to open and close them), first press and hold down the left side **shift-key** with the 4th finger of your left hand; then punch the **quotation mark** key, with the 4th finger of your right hand.*

Apostrophe   '

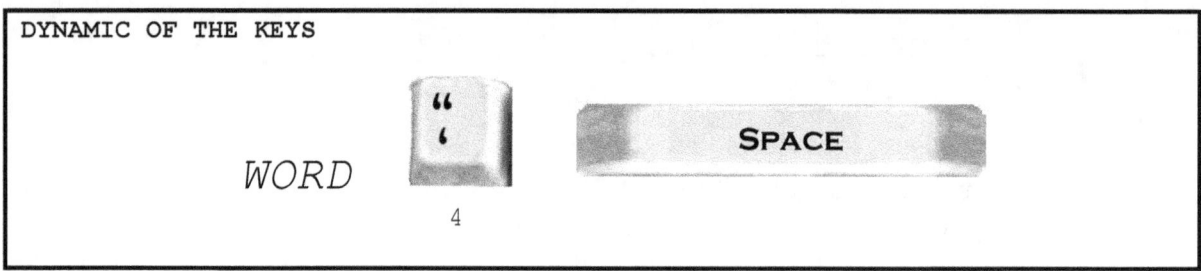

Exercise

foil' soil' toil'

Quotation Marks   " "

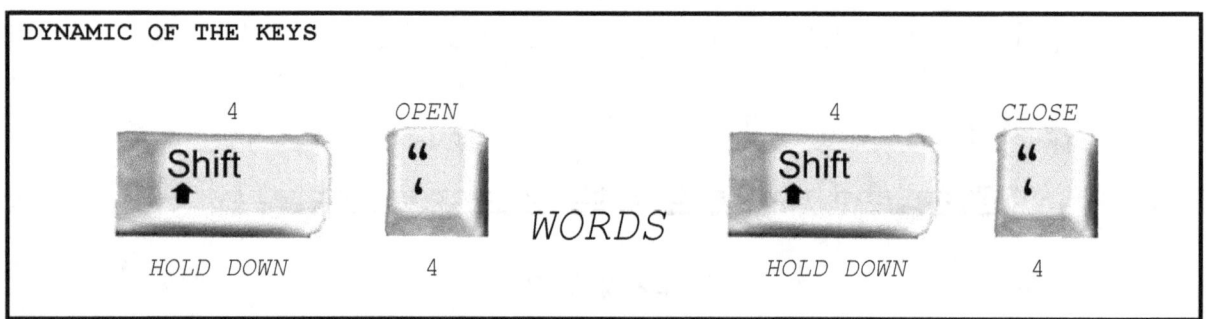

Exercise

"foil soil toil"

5th Lesson

FLAW • *DRAW* • *THAW*

Exercises

```
         1   4 3
I )      f   l a w
             3
```

II)   ff ll aa ww

III)   fff lll aaa www

IV)   ffff llll aaaa wwww

Reminders

The little numbers above and below the letters indicate the fingering, **do not type them**.

Type the letters **all the same size** using font size 20.

For complete rhythm outline see chart on **pages 17-18**, or listen to the rhythm on the Audio Instructions section of this book's **website**.

Always keep steady rhytm.

V)   f ff l ll a aa w ww

VI)   f fff l lll a aaa w www

VII)   f ffff l llll a aaaa w wwww

I)   2   1   4   3
       d   r   a   w

II)   dd   rr   aa   ww

III)   ddd   rrr   aaa   www

IV)   dddd   rrrr   aaaa   wwww

V)   d dd   r rr   a aa   w ww

VI)   d ddd   r rrr   a aaa   w www

VII)   d dddd   r rrrr   a aaaa   w wwww

          1   4   3

I)   t h a w
              1

II)   tt hh aa ww

III)   ttt hhh aaa www

IV)   tttt hhhh aaaa wwww

V)   t tt h hh a aa w ww

VI)   t ttt h hhh a aaa w www

VII)   t tttt h hhhh a aaaa w wwww

<u>Type and space the three words normally</u>

Exercise

flaw draw thaw draw thaw flaw thaw flaw draw

THE USE OF THE APOSTROPHE AND QUOTATION MARKS

Apostrophe '

DYNAMIC OF THE KEYS

WORD " ' SPACE
       4

Exercise

flaw' draw' thaw'

Quotation Marks " "

DYNAMIC OF THE KEYS

    4   OPEN   4   CLOSE
  Shift   " '   Shift   " '
 HOLD DOWN   4   WORDS   HOLD DOWN   4

Exercise

"flaw draw thaw"

6th Lesson

*FL**IP*** • *DR**IP*** • *QU**IP***

Exercises

I)   ¹f l i p
           ₃ ₂ ₄

II)   ff ll ii pp

III)   fff lll iii ppp

IV)   ffff llll iiii pppp

Reminders

The little numbers above and below the letters indicate the fingering, **do not type them**.

Type the letters **all the same size** using font size 20.

For complete rhythm outline see chart on **pages 17-18**, or listen to the rhythm on the Audio Instructions section of this book's **website**.

Always keep steady rhytm.

V)   f ff l ll i ii p pp

VI)   f fff l lll i iii p ppp

VII)   f ffff l llll i iiii p pppp

I) $\overset{2}{d}\ r\ \underset{2}{\overset{1}{i}}\ \underset{4}{p}$

II) dd rr ii pp

III) ddd rrr iii ppp

IV) dddd rrrr iiii pppp

V)   d dd r rr i ii p pp

VI) d ddd r rrr i iii p ppp

VII) d dddd r rrrr i iiii p pppp

I)   q u i p
         1 2 4
         ⁴

II)   qq uu ii pp

III) qqq uuu iii ppp

IV)   qqqq uuuu iiii pppp

V)   q qq u uu i ii p pp

VI)   q qqq u uuu i iii p ppp

VII) q qqqq u uuuu i iiii p pppp

Type and space the three words normally

Exercise

flip drip quip drip quip flip
quip flip drip

THE USE OF THE APOSTROPHE AND QUOTATION MARKS

Apostrophe   '

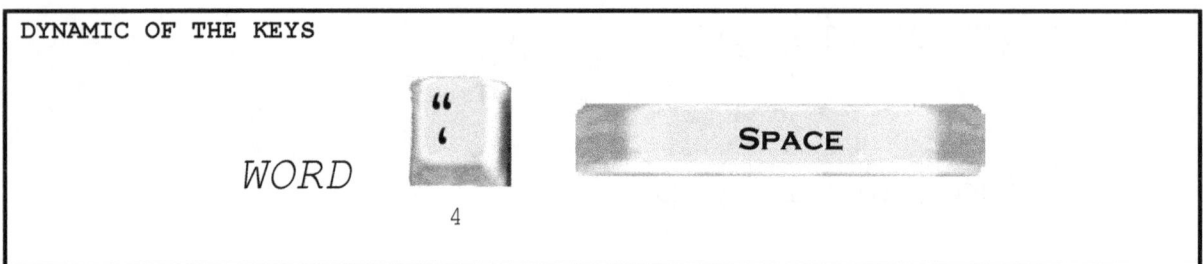

Exercise

flip' drip' quip'

Quotation Marks   " "

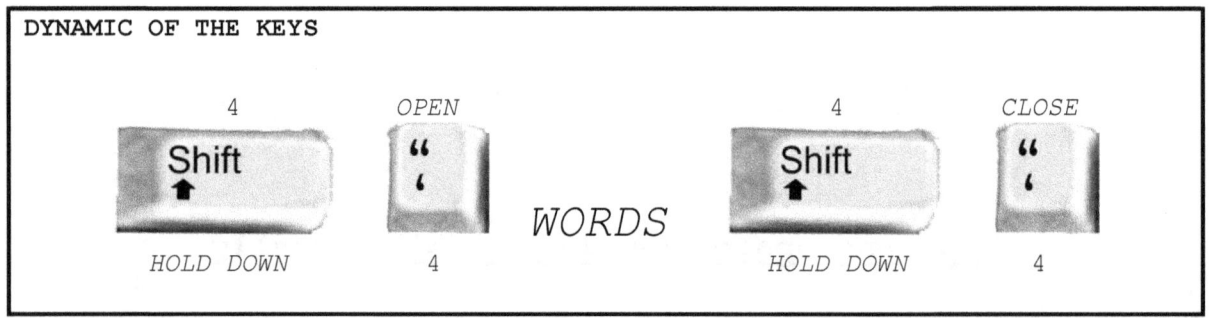

Exercise

"flip drip quip"

7th Lesson

FILE • RILE • TILE

Exercises

I)   f i l e
     (1 2 3 2)

II) ff ii ll ee

III) fff iii lll eee

IV) ffff iiii llll eeee

> **Reminders**
>
> The little numbers above and below the letters indicate the fingering, **do not type them**.
>
> Type the letters **all the same size** using font size 20.
>
> For complete rhythm outline see chart on **pages 17-18**, or listen to the rhythm on the Audio Instructions section of this book's **website**.
>
> Always keep steady rhytm.

V)   f ff i ii l ll e ee

VI) f fff i iii l lll e eee

VII) f ffff i iiii l llll e eeee

I)   r i l e
        ¹ ²
         ₂ ₃

II)   rr ii ll ee

III)   rrr iii lll eee

IV)   rrrr iiii llll eeee

V)   r rr i ii l ll e ee

VI)   r rrr i iii l lll e eee

VII)   r rrrr i iiii l llll e eeee

I)   **1**   2
     t i l e
       2 3

II) tt ii ll ee

III) ttt iii lll eee

IV) tttt iiii llll eeee

V)   t tt i ii l ll e ee

VI) t ttt i iii l lll e eee

VII) t tttt i iiii l llll e eeee

Type and space the three words normally

Exercise

file rile tile rile tile file tile file rile

THE USE OF THE COMMA AND POINTED BRACKETS

These two punctuation signs are located on the bottom row on the two keys to the right of the **M** *Key. To use the comma, just punch the* **comma** *key with the 3rd finger of your right hand. To use the* **open pointed bracket**, *first press and hold down the left side* **shift-key** *with the 4th finger of your left hand, then punch the* **open pointed bracket** *key, with the 3rd finger of your right hand. To use the* **close pointed bracket**, *first press and hold down the left side* **shift-key** *with the 4th finger of your left hand, then punch the* **close pointed bracket** *key, with the 4th finger of your right hand.*

Comma   ,

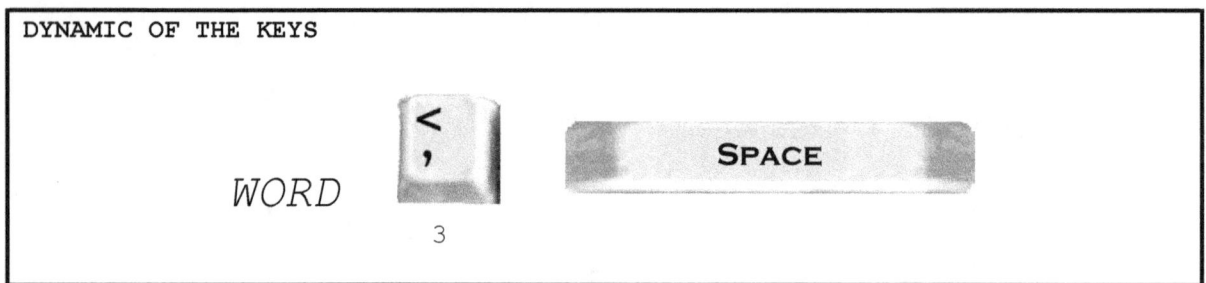

Exercise

file, rile, tile,

Pointed Brackets   <   >

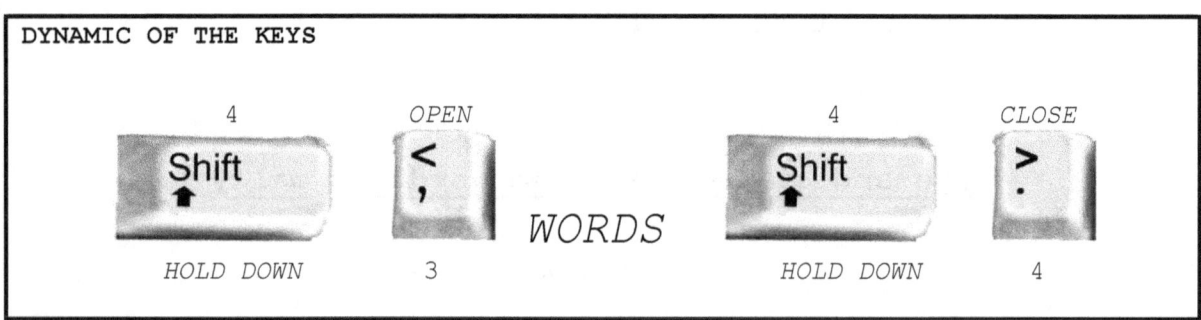

Exercise

<file rile tile>

8th Lesson

DANK • RANK • YANK

Exercises

I)   d a n k
     (2 4 / 1 2)

II) dd aa nn kk

III) ddd aaa nnn kkk

IV) dddd aaaa nnnn kkkk

V)   d dd a aa n nn k kk

VI) d ddd a aaa n nnn k kkk

VII) d dddd a aaaa n nnnn k kkkk

Reminders

The little numbers above and below the letters indicate the fingering, **do not type them**.

Type the letters **all the same size** using font size 20.

For complete rhythm outline see chart on **pages 17-18**, or listen to the rhythm on the Audio Instructions section of this book's **website**.

Always keep steady rhytm.

I)   r a n k
      ¹ ⁴
      ₁ ₂

II)   rr aa nn kk

III) rrr aaa nnn kkk

IV)   rrrr aaaa nnnn kkkk

V)   r rr a aa n nn k kk

VI)   r rrr a aaa n nnn k kkk

VII) r rrrr a aaaa n nnnn k kkkk

I)   y a n k
         ⁴
         1 1 2

II)   yy aa nn kk

III)   yyy aaa nnn kkk

IV)   yyyy aaaa nnnn kkkk

V)   y yy a aa n nn k kk

VI)   y yyy a aaa n nnn k kkk

VII)   y yyyy a aaaa n nnnn k kkkk

Type and space the three words normally

Exercise

dank rank yank rank yank dank yank dank rank

THE USE OF THE COMMA AND POINTED BRACKETS

Comma ,

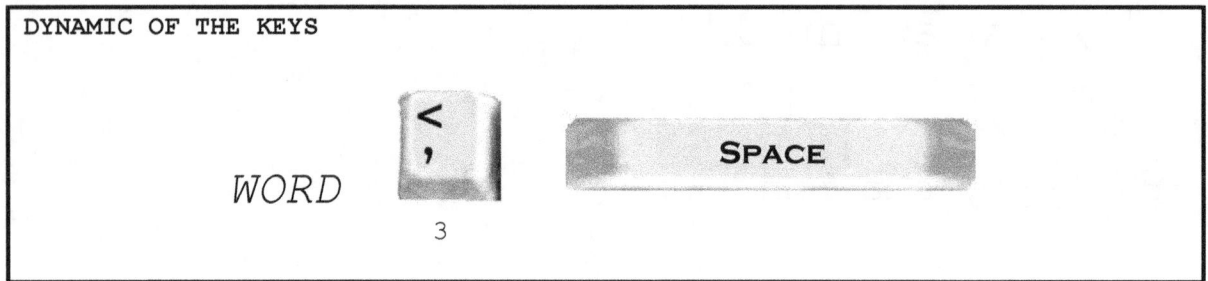

Exercise

dank, rank, yank,

Pointed Brackets < >

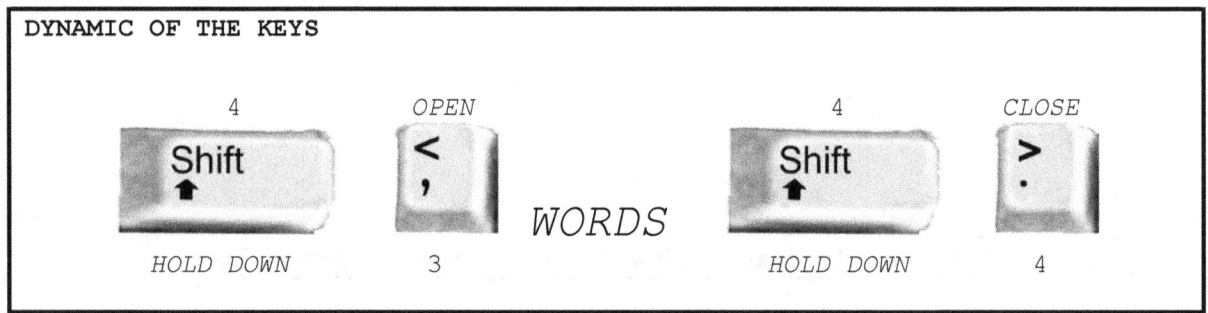

Exercise

<dank rank yank>

9th Lesson

D*OOM* • R*OOM* • Z*OOM*

Exercises

I)   d o o m
         2
       3 3 2

II)   dd oo oo mm

III) ddd ooo ooo mmm

IV)   dddd oooo oooo mmmm

V)   d dd o oo o oo m mm

VI)   d ddd o ooo o ooo m mmm

VII) d dddd o oooo o oooo m mmmm

> **Reminders**
>
> The little numbers above and below the letters indicate the fingering, **do not type them**.
>
> Type the letters **all the same size** using font size 20.
>
> For complete rhythm outline see chart on **pages 17-18**, or listen to the rhythm on the Audio Instructions section of this book's **website** .
>
> Always keep steady rhytm.

```
           1
I )     r  o  o  m
        3  3  2


II )    rr oo oo mm


III )   rrr ooo ooo mmm


IV )    rrrr oooo oooo mmmm


V )     r rr O oo O oo m mm


VI )    r rrr O ooo O ooo m mmm


VII )   r rrrr O oooo O oooo m mmmm
```

I)   z o o m
       4
     z o o m
       3 3 2

II) zz oo oo mm

III) zzz ooo ooo mmm

IV) zzzz oooo oooo mmmm

V)   z zz o oo o oo m mm

VI) z zzz o ooo o ooo m mmm

VII) z zzzz o oooo o oooo m mmmm

Type and space the three words normally

Exercise

doom room zoom room zoom doom zoom doom room

THE USE OF THE COMMA AND POINTED BRACKETS

Comma ,

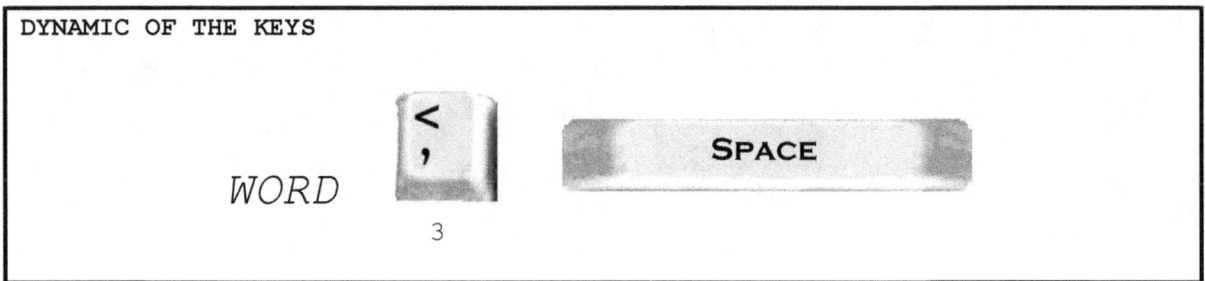

Exercise

doom, room, zoom,

Pointed Brackets < >

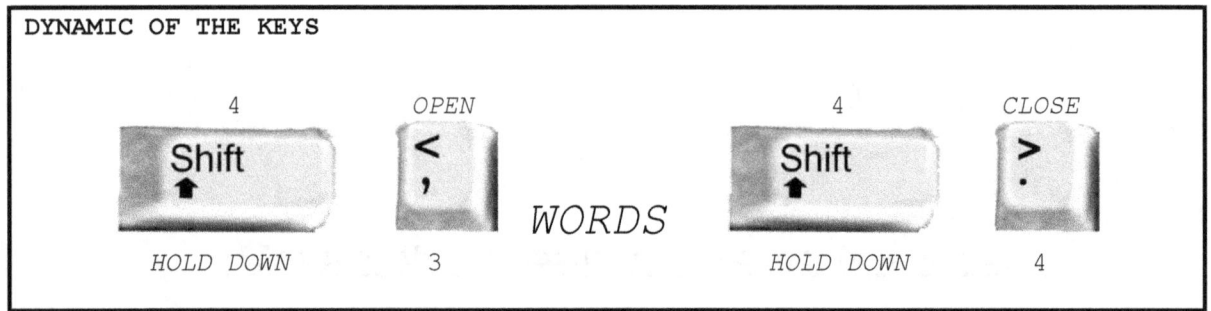

Exercise

<doom room zoom>

10th Lesson

DING • KING • ZING

Exercises

I)   ²d ¹i n g
       ₂ ₁

II) dd ii nn gg

III) ddd iii nnn ggg

IV) dddd iiii nnnn gggg

V)   d dd i ii n nn g gg

VI) d ddd i iii n nnn g ggg

VII) d dddd i iiii n nnnn g gggg

Reminders

*The little numbers above and below the letters indicate the fingering, **do not type them**.*

*Type the letters **all the same size** using font size 20.*

*For complete rhythm outline see chart on **pages 17-18**, or listen to the rhythm on the Audio Instructions section of this book's **website**.*

Always keep steady rhytm.

I)   k i n g
       2 2 1 ¹

II)   kk ii nn gg

III) kkk iii nnn ggg

IV)   kkkk iiii nnnn gggg

V)   k kk i ii n nn g gg

VI)   k kkk i iii n nnn g ggg

VII) k kkkk i iiii n nnnn g gggg

```
            4         1
I )     z   i   n   g
            2   1
```

II)   zz ii nn gg

III)   zzz iii nnn ggg

IV)   zzzz iiii nnnn gggg

V)   z zz i ii n nn g gg

VI)   z zzz i iii n nnn g ggg

VII)   z zzzz i iiii n nnnn g gggg

Type and space the three words normally

Exercise

ding king zing king zing ding zing ding king

THE USE OF THE COMMA AND POINTED BRACKETS

Comma ,

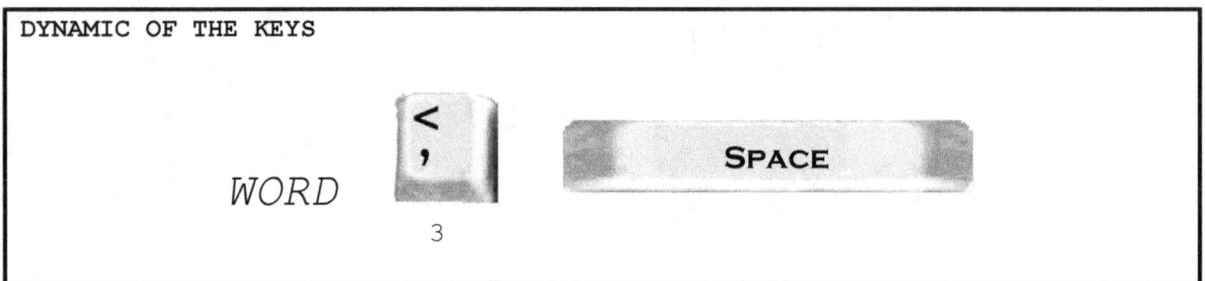

Exercise

```
ding, king, zing,
```

Pointed Brackets < >

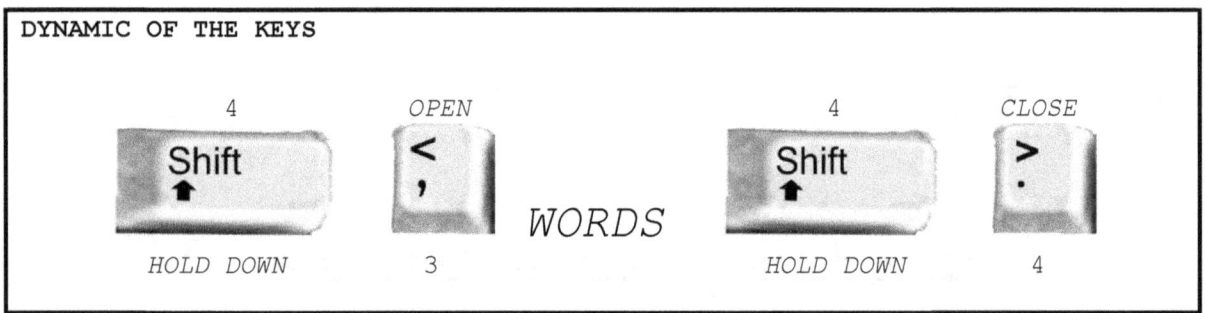

Exercise

```
<ding king zing>
```

11th Lesson

D**AMP** • V**AMP** • C**AMP**

Exercises

I)   ²   ⁴
    d a m p
       ₂   ₄

II) dd aa mm pp

III) ddd aaa mmm ppp

IV) dddd aaaa mmmm pppp

V)   d dd a aa m mm p pp

VI) d ddd a aaa m mmm p ppp

VII) d dddd a aaaa m mmmm p pppp

> **Reminders**
>
> The little numbers above and below the letters indicate the fingering, **do not type them**.
>
> Type the letters **all the same size** using font size 20.
>
> For complete rhythm outline see chart on **pages 17-18**, or listen to the rhythm on the Audio Instructions section of this book's **website**.
>
> Always keep steady rhytm.

I)   ¹   ⁴
     v a m p
        ₂   ₄

II)   vv aa mm pp

III) vvv aaa mmm ppp

IV) vvvv aaaa mmmm pppp

V)   v vv a aa m mm p pp

VI) v vvv a aaa m mmm p ppp

VII) v vvvv a aaaa m mmmm p pppp

I)   c a m p
     (2 above a, 4 above m; 2 below a, 4 below m)

II) cc aa mm pp

III) ccc aaa mmm ppp

IV) cccc aaaa mmmm pppp

V)   c cc a aa m mm p pp

VI) c ccc a aaa m mmm p ppp

VII) c cccc a aaaa m mmmm p pppp

Type and space the three words normally

Exercise

damp vamp camp vamp camp damp camp damp vamp

81

THE USE OF THE COMMA AND POINTED BRACKETS

Comma   ,

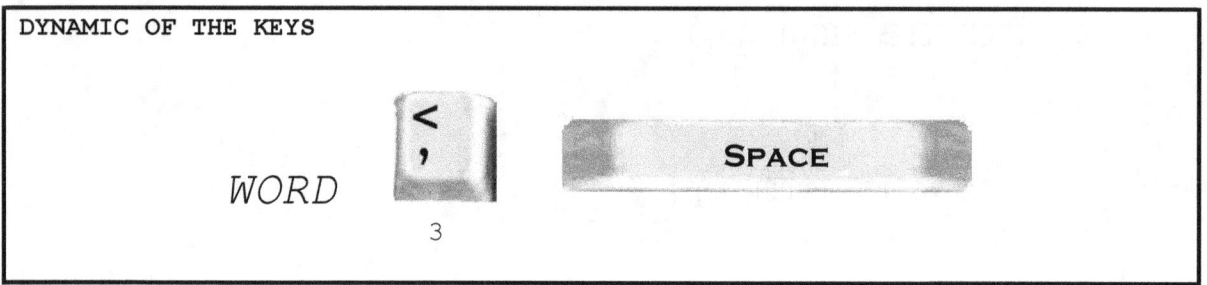

Exercise

damp, vamp, camp,

Pointed Brackets   <   >

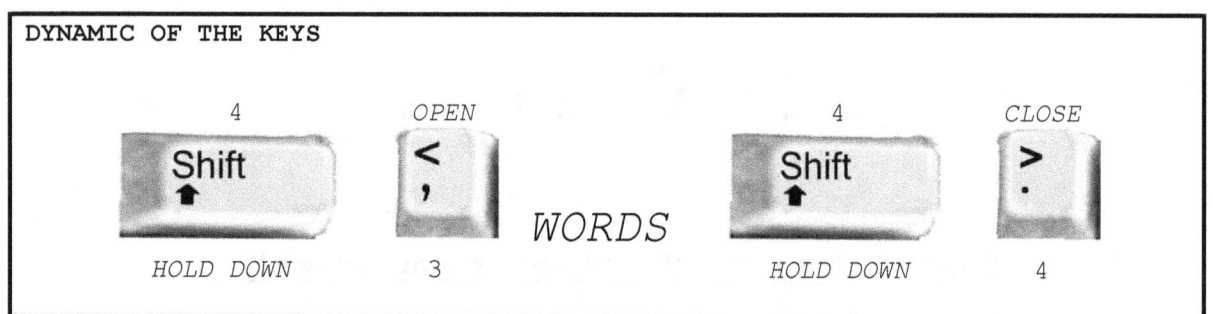

Exercise

<damp vamp camp>

12th Lesson

S**ASS** • M**ASS** • B**ASS**

Exercises

I)   3   4   3   3
      s   a   s   s

II)   ss   aa   ss   ss

III) sss   aaa   sss   sss

IV) ssss aaaa ssss ssss

Reminders

The little numbers above and below the letters indicate the fingering, **do not type them**.

Type the letters **all the same size** using font size 20.

For complete rhythm outline see chart on **pages 17-18**, or listen to the rhythm on the Audio Instructions section of this book's **website**.

Always keep steady rhytm.

V) S ss a aa S ss S ss

VI) S sss a aaa S sss S sss

VII) S ssss a aaaa S ssss S ssss

I) m a s s

4 3 3 / 2

II) mm aa ss ss

III) mmm aaa sss sss

IV) mmmm aaaa ssss ssss

V) m mm a aa s ss s ss

VI) m mmm a aaa s sss s sss

VII) m mmmm a aaaa s ssss s ssss

	1	4	3	3
I)	b	a	s	s

II)   bb aa ss ss

III)   bbb aaa sss sss

IV)   bbbb aaaa ssss ssss

V)   b bb a aa s ss s ss

VI)   b bbb a aaa s sss s sss

VII)   b bbbb a aaaa s ssss s ssss

Type and space the three words normally

Exercise

sass mass bass mass bass sass bass sass mass

THE USE OF THE PERIOD AND POINTED BRACKETS

*These two punctuation signs are located on the bottom row on the two keys to the right of the M Key. The **period** is located on the same key as the **close pointed bracket**; and the **open pointed bracket** is located on the key to the left of the **close pointed bracket** key. To use the **period**, just punch the **period** key with the 4th finger of your right hand. To use the **open pointed bracket**, first press and hold down the left side **shift-key** with the 4th finger of your left hand, then punch the **open pointed bracket** key, with the 3rd finger of your right hand. To use the **close pointed bracket**, first press and hold down the left side **shift-key** with the 4th finger of your left hand, then punch the **close pointed bracket** key, with the 4th finger of your right hand.*

Period   .

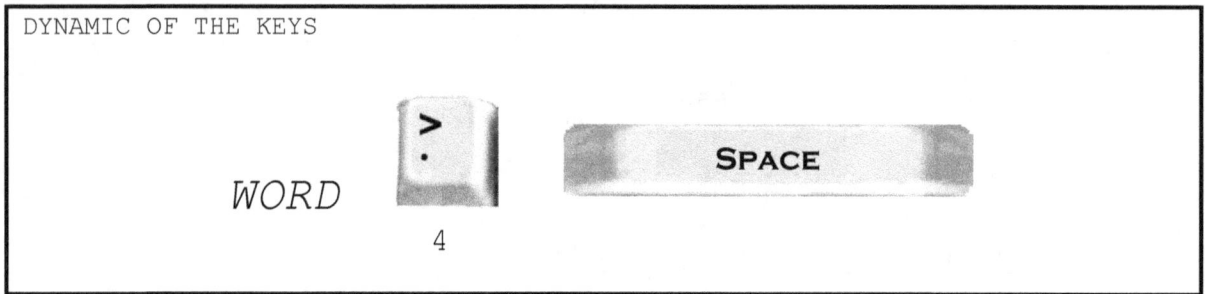

Exercise

sass. mass. bass.

Pointed Brackets   < >

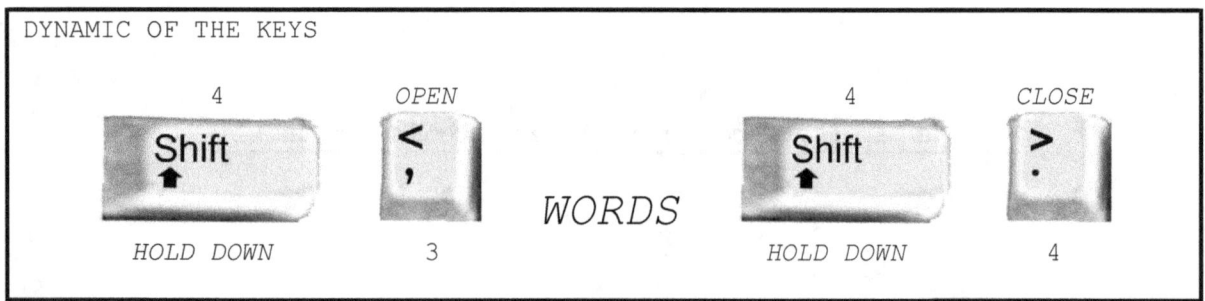

Exercise

<sass mass bass>

13th Lesson

RAGE • **W**AGE • **P**AGE

Exercises

    1   4 **1** 2

I)   r   a   g   e

II)   rr   aa   gg   ee

III)   rrr   aaa   ggg   eee

IV)   rrrr   aaaa   gggg   eeee

V)   r   rr   a   aa   g   gg   e   ee

VI)   r   rrr   a   aaa   g   ggg   e   eee

VII)   r   rrrr   a   aaaa   g   gggg   e   eeee

Reminders

*The little numbers above and below the letters indicate the fingering, **do not type them**.*

*Type the letters **all the same size** using font size 20.*

*For complete rhythm outline see chart on **pages 17-18**, or listen to the rhythm on the Audio Instructions section of this book's **website**.*

Always keep steady rhytm.

                3   4   **1**   2
I)   w   a   g   e

II)   ww   aa   gg   ee

III)   www   aaa   ggg   eee

IV)   wwww   aaaa   gggg   eeee

V)   w   ww   a   aa   g   gg   e   ee

VI)   w   www   a   aaa   g   ggg   e   eee

VII)   w   wwww   a   aaaa   g   gggg   e   eeee

I)   ⁴ **1** ²
      p a g e
      ₄

II)   pp aa gg ee

III) ppp aaa ggg eee

IV)   pppp aaaa gggg eeee

V)   p pp a aa g gg e ee

VI)   p ppp a aaa g ggg e eee

VII) p pppp a aaaa g gggg e eeee

<u>Type and space the three words normally</u>

Exercise

rage wage page wage page rage page rage wage

THE USE OF THE PERIOD AND POINTED BRACKETS

Period   .

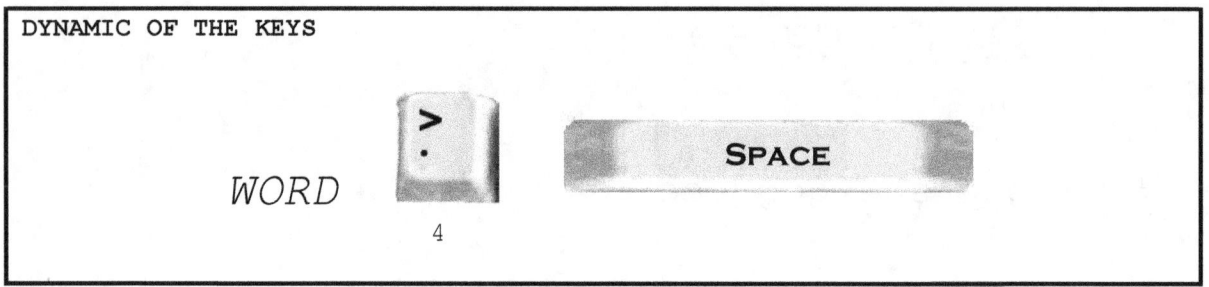

Exercise

rage. wage. page.

Pointed Brackets   <   >

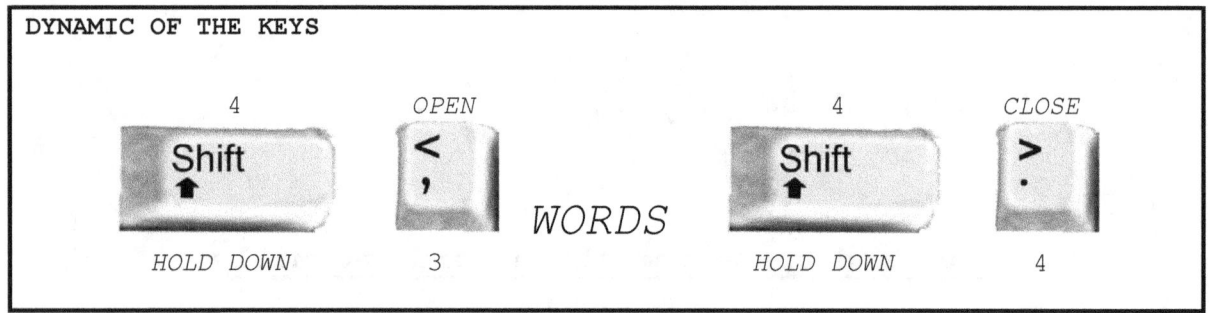

Exercise

<rage wage page>

14th Lesson

*S*IDE • *H*IDE • *R*IDE

Exercises

I)   s i d e
      (3 2 2, 2)

II)   ss ii dd ee

III) sss iii ddd eee

IV)   ssss iiii dddd eeee

V)   s ss i ii d dd e ee

VI)   s sss i iii d ddd e eee

VII) s ssss i iiii d dddd e eeee

Reminders

*The little numbers above and below the letters indicate the fingering, **do not type them**.*

*Type the letters **all the same size** using font size 20.*

*For complete rhythm outline see chart on **pages 17-18**, or listen to the rhythm on the Audio Instructions section of this book's **website**.*

Always keep steady rhytm.

I)   h i^2 d^2 e
       1 ₂

II)   hh ii dd ee

III) hhh iii ddd eee

IV)   hhhh iiii dddd eeee

V)   h hh i ii d dd e ee

VI)   h hhh i iii d ddd e eee

VII) h hhhh i iiii d dddd e eeee

92

I)   1   2 2
        r i d e
           2

II)   rr ii dd ee

III) rrr iii ddd eee

IV)   rrrr iiii dddd eeee

V)   r rr i ii d dd e ee

VI)   r rrr i iii d ddd e eee

VII) r rrrr i iiii d dddd e eeee

<u>Type and space the three words normally</u>

Exercise

side hide ride hide ride side
ride side hide

THE USE OF THE PERIOD AND POINTED BRACKETS

Period   .

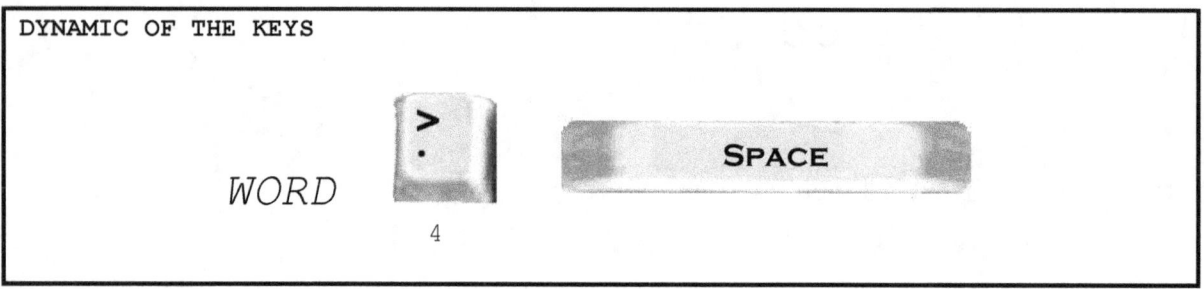

Exercise

ride. side. hide.

Pointed Brackets   <   >

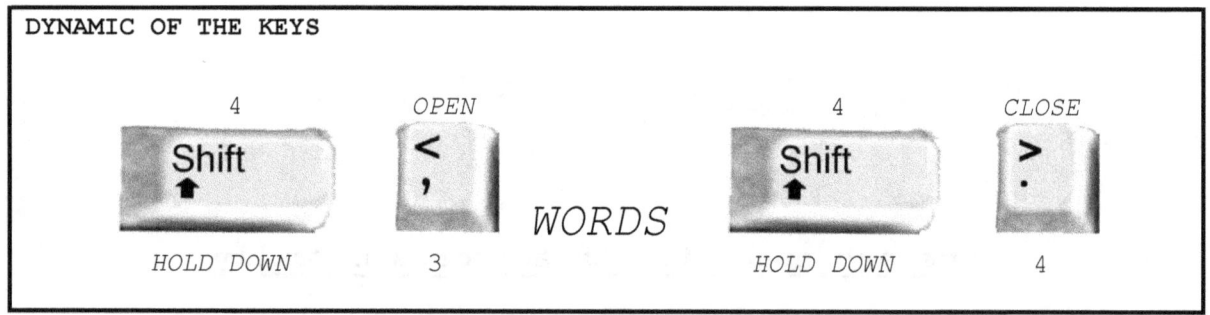

Exercise

<side hide ride>

15th Lesson

*SL**AM*** • *SC**AM*** • *EX**AM***

Exercises

I)   3 4
      s l a m
         3 2

II)   ss ll aa mm

III) sss lll aaa mmm

IV)   ssss llll aaaa mmmm

V)   s ss l ll a aa m mm

VI)   s sss l lll a aaa m mmm

VII) s ssss l llll a aaaa m mmmm

Reminders

*The little numbers above and below the letters indicate the fingering, **do not type them**.*

*Type the letters **all the same size** using font size 20.*

*For complete rhythm outline see chart on **pages 17-18**, or listen to the rhythm on the Audio Instructions section of this book's **website**.*

Always keep steady rhytm.

```
             3   2   4
I )       s   c   a   m
                 2
```

```
II )      ss  cc  aa  mm
```

```
III )     sss  ccc  aaa  mmm
```

```
IV )      ssss  cccc  aaaa  mmmm
```

```
V )       s  ss  c  cc  a  aa  m  mm
```

```
VI )      s  sss  c  ccc  a  aaa  m  mmm
```

```
VII )     s  ssss  c  cccc  a  aaaa  m  mmmm
```

```
          2   3   4
I )    e   x   a   m
                   2
```

II)   ee xx aa mm

III)   eee xxx aaa mmm

IV)   eeee xxxx aaaa mmmm

V)   e ee x xx a aa m mm

VI)   e eee x xxx a aaa m mmm

VII)   e eeee x xxxx a aaaa m mmmm

<u>Type and space the three words normally</u>

Exercise

slam scam exam scam exam slam exam slam scam

THE USE OF THE PERIOD AND POINTED BRACKETS

Period .

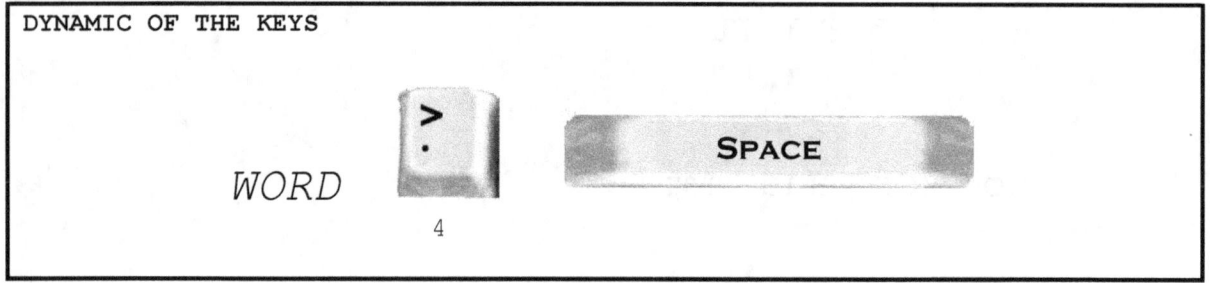

Exercise

slam. scam. exam.

Pointed Brackets < >

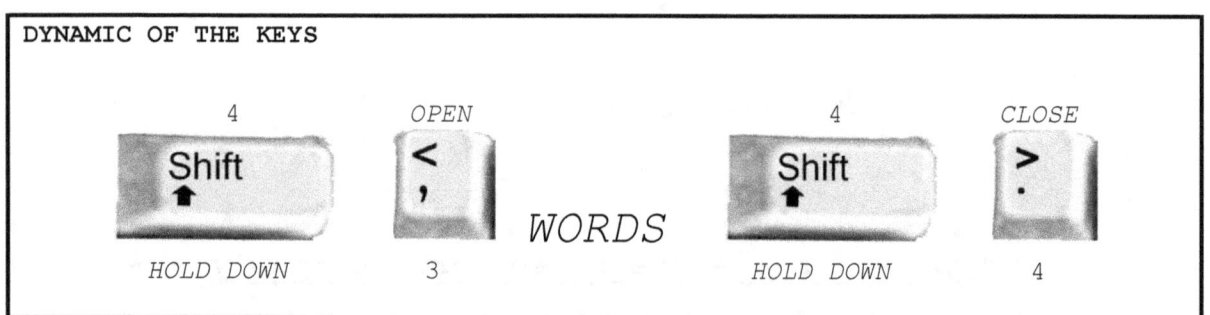

Exercise

<slam scam exam>

16th Lesson

FR**AY** • ST**AY** • AW**AY**

Exercises

I)   ¹ ¹   ⁴
      f r a y
            ₁

II) ff rr aa yy

III) fff rrr aaa yyy

IV) ffff rrrr aaaa yyyy

V) f ff r rr a aa y yy

VI) f fff r rrr a aaa y yyy

VII) f ffff r rrrr a aaaa y yyyy

Reminders

The little numbers above and below the letters indicate the fingering, **do not type them**.

Type the letters **all the same size** using font size 20.

For complete rhythm outline see chart on **pages 17-18**, or listen to the rhythm on the Audio Instructions section of this book's **website** .

Always keep steady rhytm.

I) $\overset{3}{s}\ \overset{\mathbf{1}}{t}\ \overset{4}{a}\ \underset{\mathbf{1}}{y}$

II)   ss tt aa yy

III)   sss ttt aaa yyy

IV)   ssss tttt aaaa yyyy

V)   s ss t tt a aa y yy

VI)   s sss t ttt a aaa y yyy

VII)   s ssss t tttt a aaaa y yyyy

100

```
              4   3   4
I )        a  w   a   y
                       1
```

II)   aa ww aa yy

III)   aaa www aaa yyy

IV)   aaaa wwww aaaa yyyy

V)   a aa w ww a aa y yy

VI)   a aaa w www a aaa y yyy

VII)   a aaaa w wwww a aaaa y yyyy

Type and space the three words normally

Exercise

fray stay away stay away fray away fray stay

THE USE OF THE PERIOD AND POINTED BRACKETS

Period   .

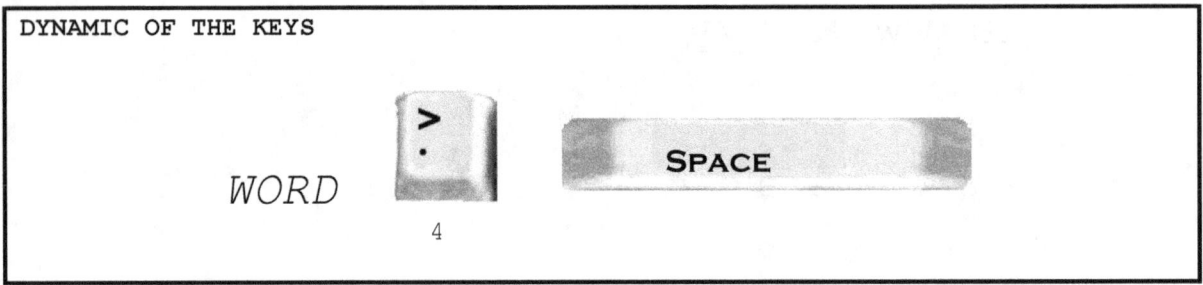

Exercise

`fray. stay. away.`

Pointed Brackets   < >

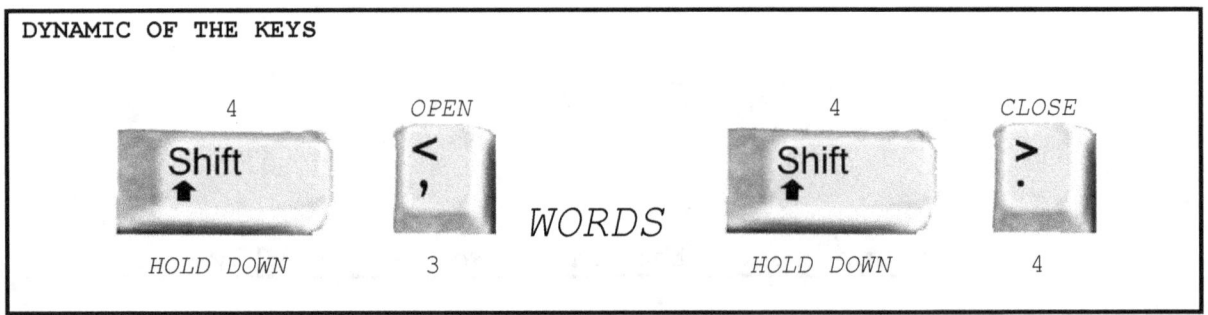

Exercise

`<fray stay away>`

17th Lesson

AJ**AR** • ST**AR** • CZ**AR**

Exercises

I) a j a r (4 4 1, 1 under j)

II) aa jj aa rr

III) aaa jjj aaa rrr

IV) aaaa jjjj aaaa rrrr

V) a aa j jj a aa r rr

VI) a aaa j jjj a aaa r rrr

VII) a aaaa j jjjj a aaaa r rrrr

Reminders

The little numbers above and below the letters indicate the fingering, **do not type them**.

Type the letters **all the same size** using font size 20.

For complete rhythm outline see chart on **pages 17-18**, or listen to the rhythm on the Audio Instructions section of this book's **website**.

Always keep steady rhytm.

103

```
         3  1  4  1
  I)     s  t  a  r


  II)    ss  tt  aa  rr


  III)   sss  ttt  aaa  rrr


  IV)    ssss  tttt  aaaa  rrrr


  V)     s  ss  t  tt  a  aa  r  rr


  VI)    s  sss  t  ttt  a  aaa  r  rrr


  VII)   s  ssss  t  tttt  a  aaaa  r  rrrr
```

```
         2   4   4   1
I)     c   z   a   r


II)    cc  zz  aa  rr


III)   ccc zzz aaa rrr


IV)    cccc zzzz aaaa rrrr


V)     c cc  z zz  a aa  r rr


VI)    c ccc  z zzz  a aaa  r rrr


VII)   c cccc  z zzzz  a aaaa  r rrrr
```

Type and space the three words normally

Exercise

ajar star czar star czar ajar czar ajar star

THE USE OF THE SLASH AND QUESTION MARK

*These two punctuation signs are located on the bottom row on key just to the right of the period Key. To use the **slash**, just punch that key with the 4th finger of your right hand. To use the **question mark**, first press and hold down the left side **shift-key** with the 4th finger of your left hand, then punch the **question mark** key, with the 4th finger of your right hand.*

Slash   /

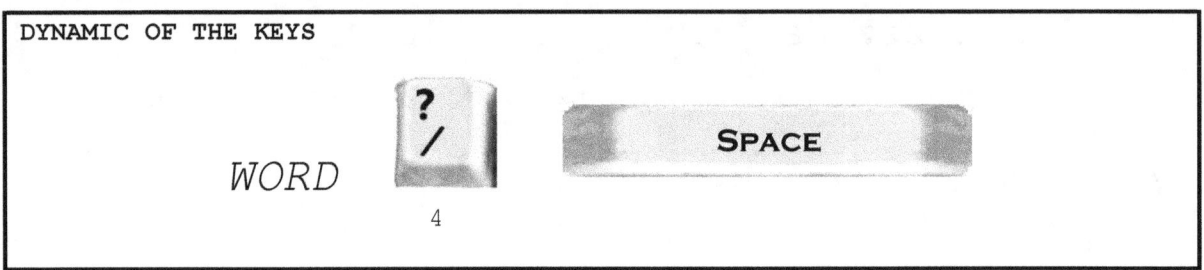

Exercise

ajar/ star/ czar/

Question Mark   ?

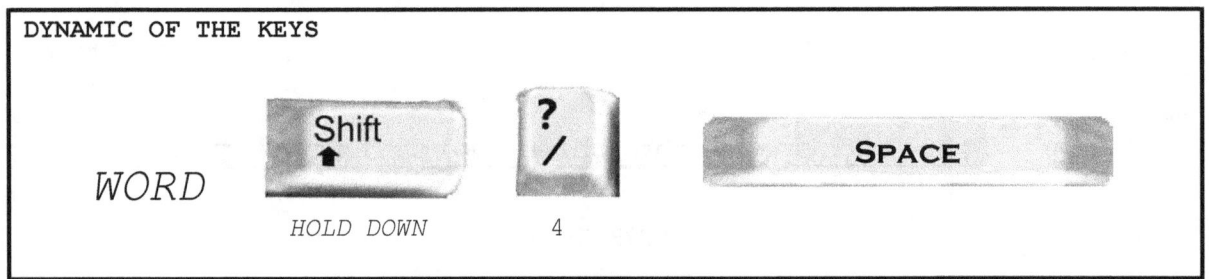

Exercise

ajar? star? czar?

18th Lesson

GOOP • *LOOP* • *POOP*

Exercises

I)   **1**
      g o o p
         3 3 4

II) gg oo oo pp

III) ggg ooo ooo ppp

IV) gggg oooo oooo pppp

> **Reminders**
>
> *The little numbers above and below the letters indicate the fingering, **do not type them**.*
>
> *Type the letters **all the same size** using font size 20.*
>
> *For complete rhythm outline see chart on **pages 17-18**, or listen to the rhythm on the Audio Instructions section of this book's **website**.*
>
> *Always keep steady rhytm.*

V)   g gg o oo o oo p pp

VI) g ggg o ooo o ooo p ppp

VII) g gggg o oooo o oooo p pppp

I)   l   o   o   p
        3   3   3   4

II)   ll oo oo pp

III)   lll ooo ooo ppp

IV)   llll oooo oooo pppp

V)   l ll o oo o oo p pp

VI)   l lll o ooo o ooo p ppp

VII)   l llll o oooo o oooo p pppp

I)   p   o   o   p
     4   3   3   4

II) pp oo oo pp

III) ppp ooo ooo ppp

IV) pppp oooo oooo pppp

V)   p pp o oo o oo p pp

VI) p ppp o ooo o ooo p ppp

VII) p pppp o oooo o oooo p pppp

<u>Type and space the three words normally</u>

Exercise

goop loop poop loop poop goop poop goop loop

THE USE OF THE SLASH AND QUESTION MARK

Slash   /

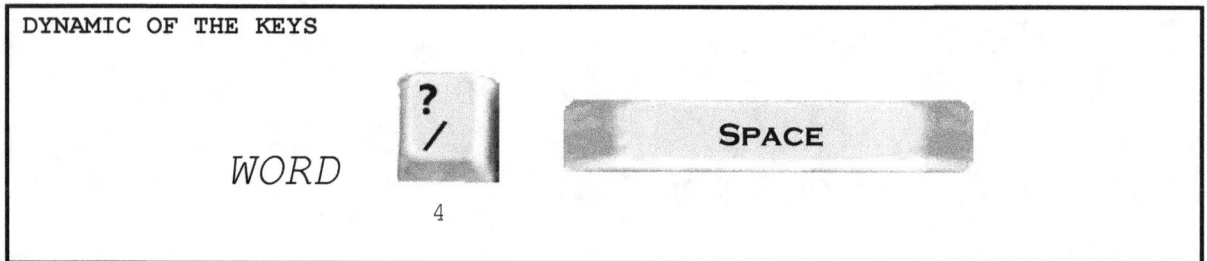

Exercise

goop/ loop/ poop/

Question Mark   ?

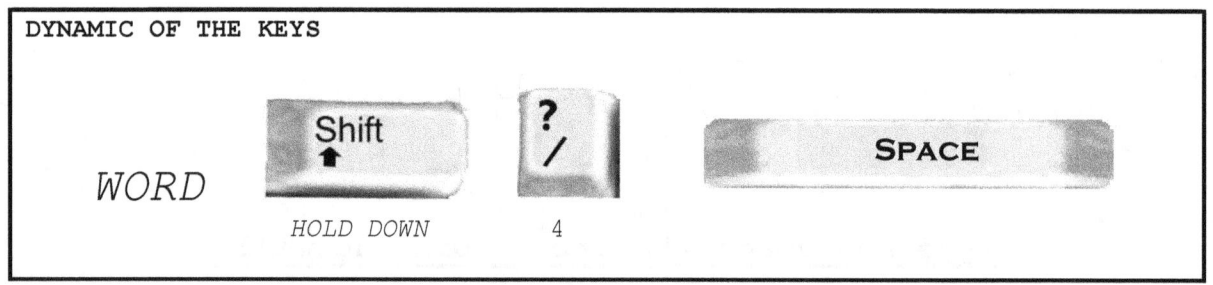

Exercise

goop? loop? loop?

19ᵗʰ Lesson

GAIN • VAIN • RAIN

Exercises

1   4
I)   g a i n
          2   1

II)   gg aa ii nn

III)   ggg aaa iii nnn

IV)   gggg aaaa iiii nnnn

V)   g gg a aa i ii n nn

VI)   g ggg a aaa i iii n nnn

VII)   g gggg a aaaa i iiii n nnnn

> **Reminders**
>
> The little numbers above and below the letters indicate the fingering, **do not type them**.
>
> Type the letters **all the same size** using font size 20.
>
> For complete rhythm outline see chart on **pages 17-18**, or listen to the rhythm on the Audio Instructions section of this book's **website** .
>
> Always keep steady rhytm.

I)   ¹   ⁴
       v a i n
           ₂ ₁

II)   vv aa ii nn

III)   vvv aaa iii nnn

IV)   vvvv aaaa iiii nnnn

V)   v vv a aa i ii n nn

VI)   v vvv a aaa i iii n nnn

VII)   v vvvv a aaaa i iiii n nnnn

I) 	 1 4

       r a i n

          2 1

II)   rr aa ii nn

III) rrr aaa iii nnn

IV)   rrrr aaaa iiii nnnn

V)   r rr a aa i ii n nn

VI)   r rrr a aaa i iii n nnn

VII) r rrrr a aaaa i iiii n nnnn

Type and space the three words normally

Exercise

gain vain rain vain rain gain rain gain vain

THE USE OF THE SLAH AND QUESTION MARK

Slash /

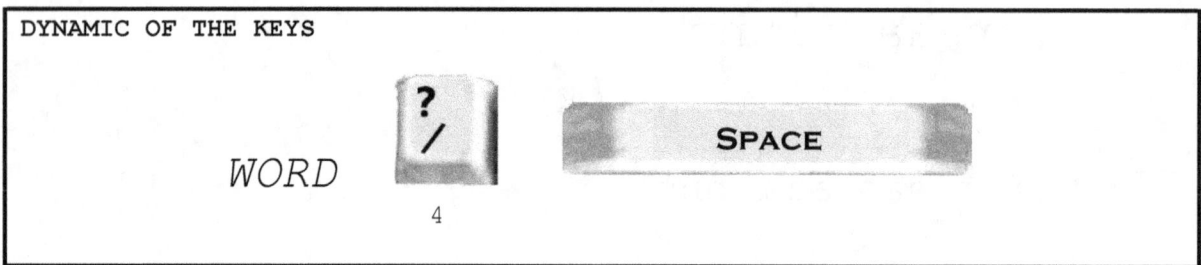

Exercise

gain/ vain/ rain/

Question Mark ?

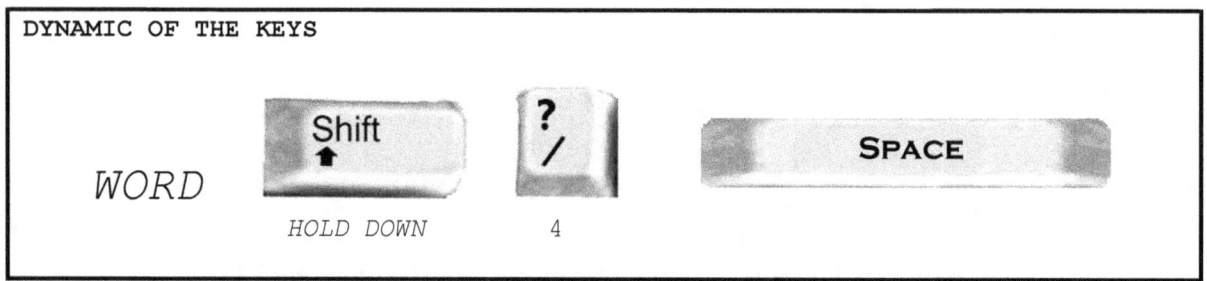

Exercise

gain? vain? rain?

20th Lesson

J*ACK* • H*ACK* • S*ACK*

Exercises

I)   j a c k
      (1 4 2 2)

II) jj aa cc kk

III) jjj aaa ccc kkk

IV) jjjj aaaa cccc kkkk

> **Reminders**
>
> The little numbers above and below the letters indicate the fingering, **do not type them**.
>
> Type the letters **all the same size** using font size 20.
>
> For complete rhythm outline see chart on **pages 17-18**, or listen to the rhythm on the Audio Instructions section of this book's **website**.
>
> Always keep steady rhytm.

V)   j jj a aa c cc k kk

VI) j jjj a aaa c ccc k kkk

VII) j jjjj a aaaa c cccc k kkkk

I)   h⁴ a² c k
      1   2

II)   hh aa cc kk

III) hhh aaa ccc kkk

IV)   hhhh aaaa cccc kkkk

V)   h hh a aa c cc k kk

VI)   h hhh a aaa c ccc k kkk

VII) h hhhh a aaaa c cccc k kkkk

```
          3   4   2
I )     s   a   c   k
                    2
```

```
II )    ss  aa  cc  kk
```

```
III )   sss  aaa  ccc  kkk
```

```
IV )    ssss  aaaa  cccc  kkkk
```

```
V )     s ss  a aa  c cc  k kk
```

```
VI )    s sss  a aaa  c ccc  k kkk
```

```
VII )   s ssss  a aaaa  c cccc  k kkkk
```

Type and space the three words normally

Exercise

jack hack sack hack sack jack
sack jack hack

THE USE OF THE SQUARE AND CURLY BRACKETS

These two punctuation signs are located on the top row on the two keys to the right of the **P** *key. To use the* **open square bracket**, *just punch the* **open square bracket** *key with the 4th finger of your right hand; to use the* **open braces**, *first press and hold down the left side* **shift-key** *with the 4th finger of your left hand, then punch that key, with the 4th finger of your right hand. To use the* **close square bracket**, *just punch the* **close square bracket** *key with the 4th finger of your right hand; to use the* **close braces**, *first press and hold down the left side* **shift-key** *with the 4th finger of your left hand, then punch that key, with the 4th finger of your right hand.*

Square Brackets   [   ]

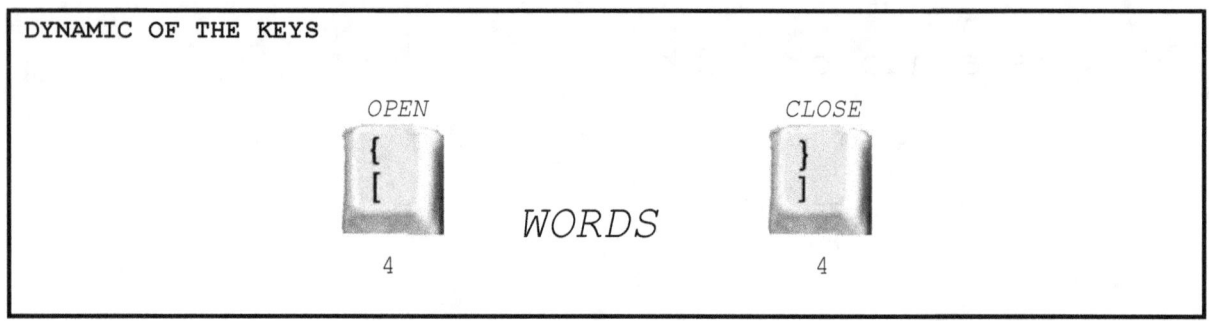

Exercise

[jack hack sack]

Curly Brackets   {   }

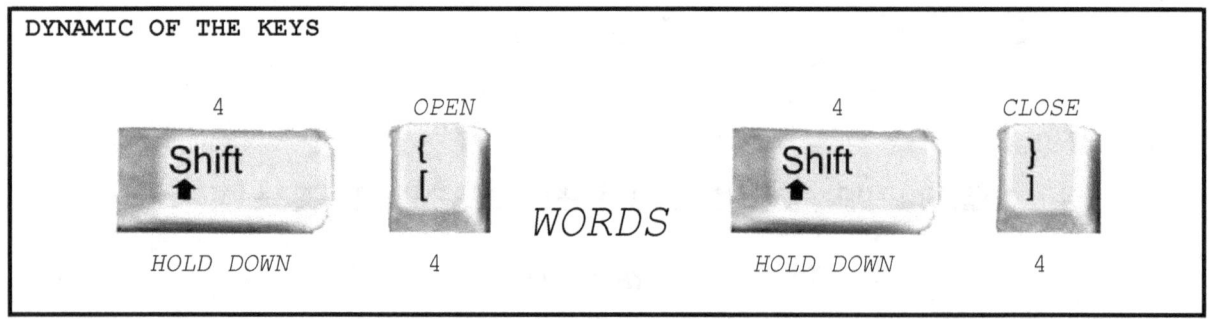

Exercise

{jack hack sack}

21ˢᵗ Lesson

JADE • FADE • WADE

Exercises

I) j a d e
    (4 2 2, 1)

II) jj aa dd ee

III) jjj aaa ddd eee

IV) jjjj aaaa dddd eeee

V) j jj a aa d dd e ee

VI) j jjj a aaa d ddd e eee

VII) j jjjj a aaaa d dddd e eeee

Reminders

The little numbers above and below the letters indicate the fingering, **do not type them**.

Type the letters **all the same size** using font size 20.

For complete rhythm outline see chart on **pages 17-18**, or listen to the rhythm on the Audio Instructions section of this book's **website**.

Always keep steady rhytm.

```
            1   4   2   2
  I )      f   a   d   e


 II )      ff  aa  dd  ee


III )      fff aaa ddd eee


 IV )      ffff aaaa dddd eeee


  V )      f ff  a aa  d dd  e ee


 VI )      f fff  a aaa  d ddd  e eee


VII )      f ffff  a aaaa  d dddd  e eeee
```

```
                3  4  2  2
I )      w  a  d  e


II )     ww  aa  dd  ee


III )    www  aaa  ddd  eee


IV )     wwww  aaaa  dddd  eeee


V )      w  ww  a  aa  d  dd  e  ee


VI )     w  www  a  aaa  d  ddd  e  eee


VII )    w  wwww  a  aaaa  d  dddd  e  eeee
```

Type and space the three words normally

Exercise

jade fade wade fade wade jade
wade jade fade

THE USE OF THE SQUARE AND CURLY BRACKETS

Square Brackets   [   ]

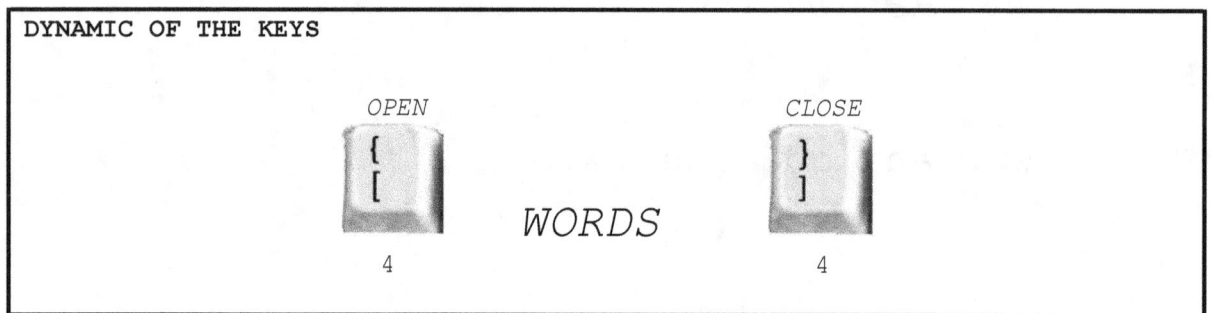

Exercise

[jade fade wade]

Curly Brackets   {   }

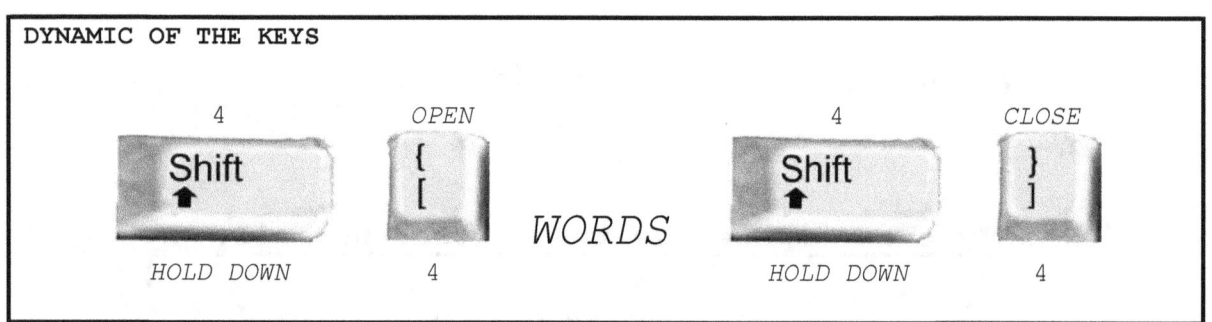

Exercise

{jade fade wade}

22ⁿᵈ Lesson

KILL • FILL • DILL

Exercises

I) k i l l
    2 2 3 3

II) kk ii ll ll

III) kkk iii lll lll

IV) kkkk iiii llll llll

> **Reminders**
>
> *The little numbers above and below the letters indicate the fingering, **do not type them**.*
>
> *Type the letters **all the same size** using font size 20.*
>
> *For complete rhythm outline see chart on **pages 17-18**, or listen to the rhythm on the Audio Instructions section of this book's **website**.*
>
> *Always keep steady rhytm.*

V) k kk i ii l ll l ll

VI) k kkk i iii l lll l lll

VII) k kkkk i iiii l llll l llll

123

I)   f i l l
      ¹
      2 3 3

II)   ff ii ll ll

III) fff iii lll lll

IV)   ffff iiii llll llll

V)   f ff i ii l ll l ll

VI)   f fff i iii l lll l lll

VII) f ffff i iiii l llll l llll

I)   d i l l
       2
      2 3 3

II)   dd ii ll ll

III) ddd iii lll lll

IV)   dddd iiii llll llll

V)   d dd i ii l ll l ll

VI)   d ddd i iii l lll l lll

VII) d dddd i iiii l llll l llll

Type and space the three words normally

Exercise

kill fill dill fill dill kill
dill kill fill

THE USE OF THE SQUARE AND CURLY BRACKETS

Square Brackets   [   ]

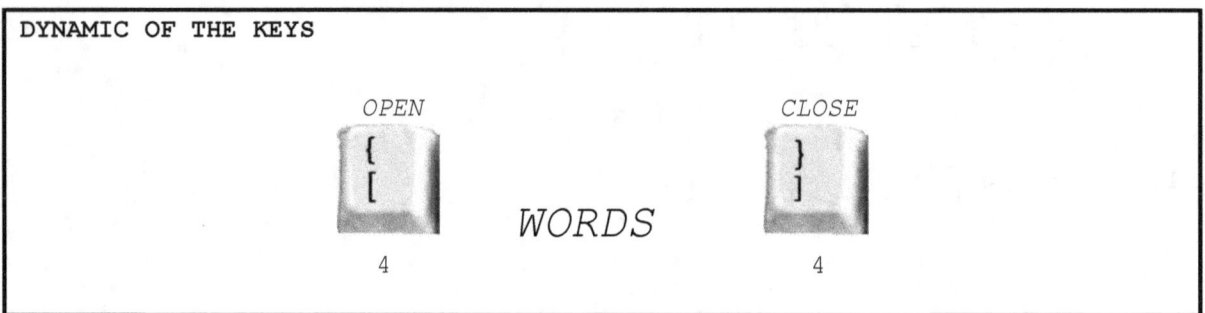

Exercise

`[kill fill dill]`

Curly Brackets   {   }

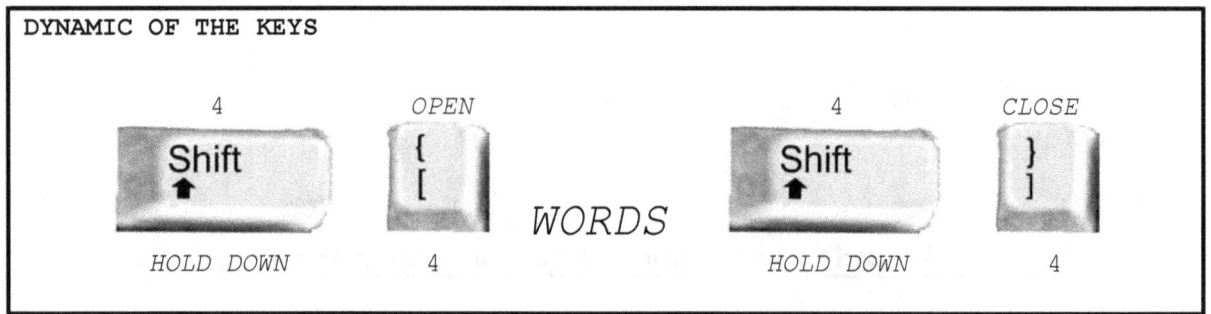

Exercise

`{kill fill dill}`

23rd Lesson

LICE • *VICE* • *NICE*

Exercises

I)   l i c e

II)   ll ii cc ee

III)   lll iii ccc eee

IV)   llll iiii cccc eeee

Reminders

*The little numbers above and below the letters indicate the fingering, **do not type them**.*

*Type the letters **all the same size** using font size 20.*

*For complete rhythm outline see chart on **pages 17-18**, or listen to the rhythm on the Audio Instructions section of this book's **website**.*

Always keep steady rhytm.

V)   l ll i ii c cc e ee

VI)   l lll i iii c ccc e eee

VII)   l llll i iiii c cccc e eeee

I)   v i c e
        1 2 2
          2

II)   vv ii cc ee

III)   vvv iii ccc eee

IV)   vvvv iiii cccc eeee

V)   v vv i ii c cc e ee

VI)   v vvv i iii c ccc e eee

VII)   v vvvv i iiii c cccc e eeee

I)   n i c e
         ² ²
     ₁ ₂

II) nn ii cc ee

III) nnn iii ccc eee

IV) nnnn iiii cccc eeee

V)   n nn i ii c cc e ee

VI) n nnn i iii c ccc e eee

VII) n nnnn i iiii c cccc e eeee

Type and space the three words normally

Exercise

lice vice nice vice nice lice
nice lice vice

THE USE OF THE BACKSLASH AND VERTICAL BAR

These two punctuation signs are located on the top row on key just to the right of the **square bracket** *Keys. To use the* **slant,** *just punch that key with the 4th finger of your right hand. To use the* **vertical bar,** *first press and hold down the left side* **shift-key** *with the 4th finger of your left hand, then punch the* **vertical bar** *key, with the 4th finger of your right hand.*

Backslash   \

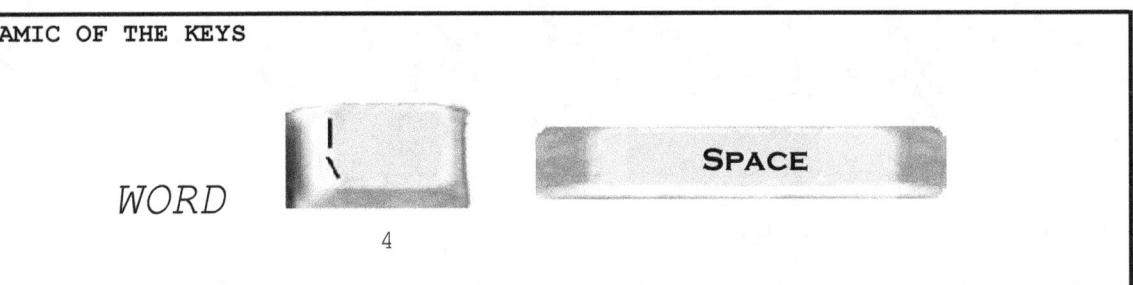

Exercise

lice\ vice\ nice\

Vertical Bar |

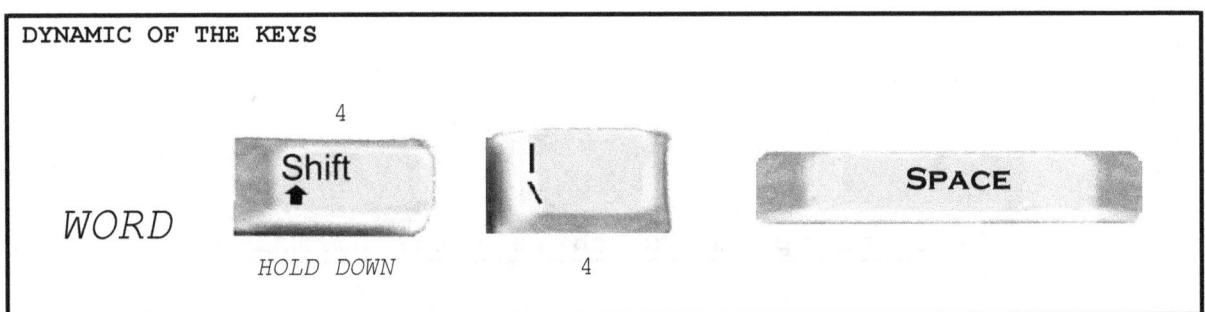

Exercise

lice | vice | nice |

130

24ᵗʰ Lesson

*P****UFF*** • *C****UFF*** • *B****UFF***

Exercises

I)   p u f f
         (fingering: 1 1 above f f; 4 1 below p u)

II) pp uu ff ff

III) ppp uuu fff fff

IV) pppp uuuu ffff ffff

V)   p pp u uu f ff f ff

VI) p ppp u uuu f fff f fff

VII) p pppp u uuuu f ffff f ffff

Reminders

The little numbers above and below the letters indicate the fingering, **do not type them**.

Type the letters **all the same size** using font size 20.

For complete rhythm outline see chart on **pages 17-18**, or listen to the rhythm on the Audio Instructions section of this book's **website**.

Always keep steady rhytm.

I)   c u f f
     ² ¹ ¹
       ₁

II) cc uu ff ff

III) ccc uuu fff fff

IV) cccc uuuu ffff ffff

V)   c cc u uu f ff f ff

VI) c ccc u uuu f fff f fff

VII) c cccc u uuuu f ffff f ffff

I)   **b** ¹u ¹f ¹f
     ₁

II) bb uu ff ff

III) bbb uuu fff fff

IV) bbbb uuuu ffff ffff

V)   b bb u uu f ff f ff

VI) b bbb u uuu f fff f fff

VII) b bbbb u uuuu f ffff f ffff

Type and space the three words normally

Exercise

puff cuff buff cuff buff puff buff puff cuff

THE USE OF THE BACKSLASH AND VERTICAL BAR

Backslash \

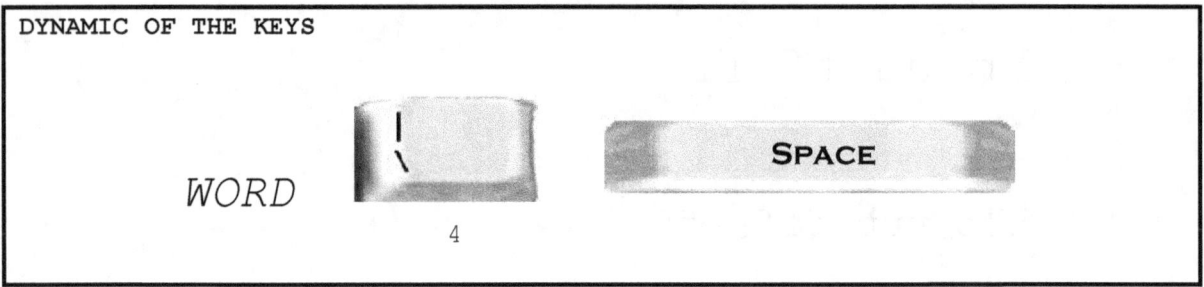

Exercise

puff\ cuff\ buff\

Vertical Bar |

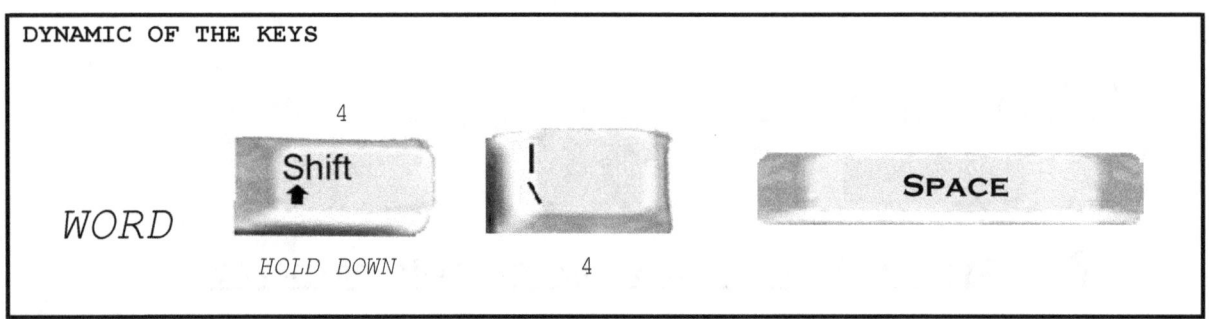

Exercise

puff | cuff | buff |

25th Lesson

H**ARD** • B**ARD** • Y**ARD**

Exercises

          4 1 2

I)   h a r d
       1

II) hh aa rr dd

III) hhh aaa rrr ddd

IV) hhhh aaaa rrrr dddd

> **Reminders**
>
> *The little numbers above and below the letters indicate the fingering, **do not type them**.*
>
> *Type the letters **all the same size** using font size 20.*
>
> *For complete rhythm outline see chart on **pages 17-18**, or listen to the rhythm on the Audio Instructions section of this book's **website** .*
>
> *Always keep steady rhytm.*

V) h hh a aa r rr d dd

VI) h hhh a aaa r rrr d ddd

VII) h hhhh a aaaa r rrrr d dddd

	1 4 1 2

I)   b a r d

II)   bb aa rr dd

III)   bbb aaa rrr ddd

IV)   bbbb aaaa rrrr dddd

V)   b bb a aa r rr d dd

VI)   b bbb a aaa r rrr d ddd

VII)   b bbbb a aaaa r rrrr d dddd

I)   y⁴ a¹ r² d
        ₁

II)   yy aa rr dd

III)   yyy aaa rrr ddd

IV)   yyyy aaaa rrrr dddd

V)   y yy a aa r rr d dd

VI)   y yyy a aaa r rrr d ddd

VII)   y yyyy a aaaa r rrrr d dddd

Type and space the three words normally

Exercise

hard bard yard bard yard hard yard hard bard

THE USE OF THE BACKSLASH AND VERTICAL BAR

Backslash \

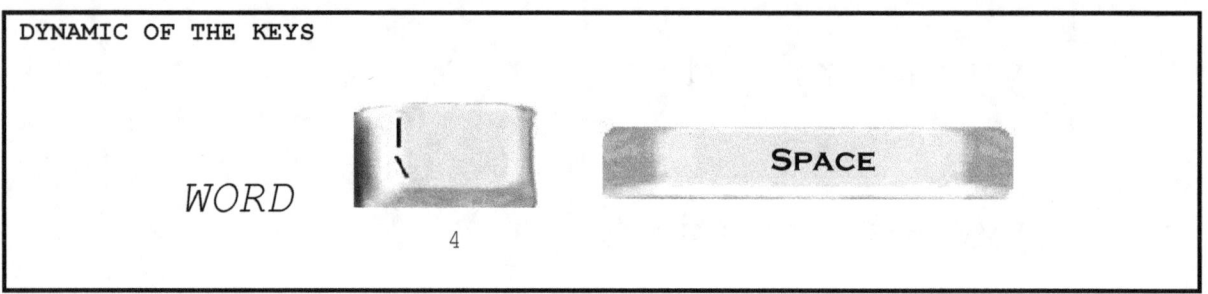

Exercise

hard\ bard\ yard\

Vertical Bar |

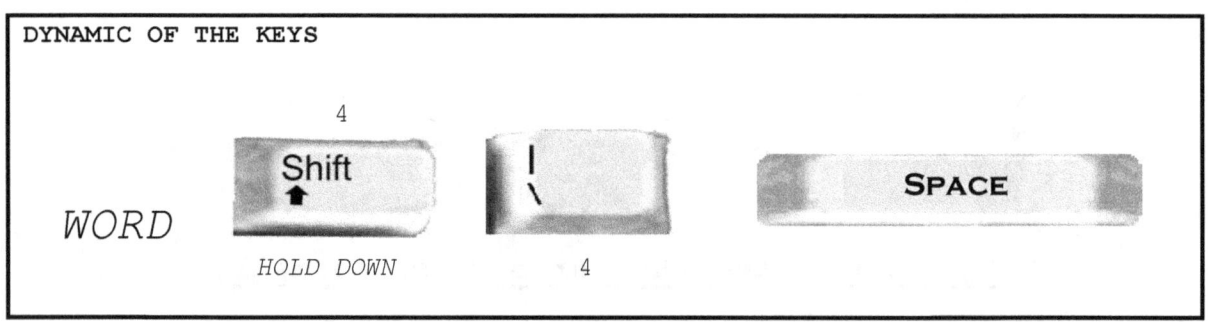

Exercise

hard | bard | yard |

Advanced Practice on all the Words in the 25 Lessons

Reminder

*Type the letters **all the same size** using font size 20.*

Exercises

1) *4 Seconds* fall fall *1 Sec.*   *4 Seconds* gall gall *1 Sec.*   *4 Seconds* hall hall *1 Sec.*

2) flag flag drag drag shag shag

3) flee flee glee glee free free

4) foil foil soil soil toil toil

5) flaw flaw draw draw thaw thaw

6) flip flip drip drip quip quip

7) file file rile rile tile tile

8) dank dank rank rank yank yank

9) doom doom room room zoom zoom

10) ding ding king king zing zing

11) damp damp vamp vamp camp camp

12) sass sass mass mass bass bass

13) rage rage wage wage page page

14) side side hide hide ride ride

15) slam slam scam scam exam exam

16) fray fray stay stay away away

17) ajar ajar star star czar czar

18) goop goop loop loop poop poop

19) gain gain vain vain rain rain

20) jack jack hack hack sack sack

21) jade jade fade fade wade wade

22) kill kill fill fill dill dill

23) lice lice vice vice nice nice

24) puff puff cuff cuff buff buff

25) hard hard bard bard yard yard

Part Three

Practice on Sentences

Every word used in this section as sentences and in the next section as paragraphs, expressed in the form of proverbs, is no more than four letters long. Type each proverb normally, not necessarily with the strict rhythm used in the exercises of the 25 lessons, yet always in a rhythmical mode as explained on page 144.

In the practice of these sentences, first read an entire Proverb and memorize it, then type it down three times.

> Type the sentences free of rhythm in the same format as it appears.

Exercises

All is fair in love.

No news is good news.

Any dog has its day.

Love me love my dog.

Big bird, don't eat rice.

You reap what you sow.

What is done is done.

Good wife, care free life.

You get what you pay for.

A good man won't beat his wife.

When no one begs all are even.

If you can't beat them, join them.

Do as I say not as I do.

A miss is as good as a mile.

Work hard and the job is half done.

Cats that love to purr don't hunt mice.

One mind can't be put to two uses.

You can't have your cake and eat it too.

Good has its gain, and evil has its cost.

When the cat is away the mice will play.

Wine can make you win or make you fail.

Buy dry wood and you will burn your pot.

If the gain is big, the risk is big.

Man may die for gold; bird may die for food.

Don't take from the poor; don't rely on the rich.

A fall in the pit is a gain of your wit.

A good name is hard to gain but easy to lose.

If you don't do bad acts, you will fear no harm.

If the old is not gone, then the new will not come.

If a man does not keep his word, what good is he?

A bird in the hand is as good as two in the bush.

Practice on Paragraphs

Type the paragraphs free of rhythm in the same format as it appears.

Exercises

   All is fair in love. No news is good news. Any dog has its day. What is done is done. Love me, love my dog. Big bird, don't eat rice. Do as I say, not as I do. You reap what you sow.

   Good wife, care free life. You get what you pay for. A miss is as good as a mile. If the gain is big, the risk is big. A good man won't beat his wife. If you can't beat them, join them. A fall in the pit is a gain in your wit. One mind can't be put to two uses. When no one begs then all are even. Work hard and the job is half done.

   You can't have your cake and eat it too. Good has its gain, and evil has its cost. Cats that love to purr don't hunt mice. When the cat is away the mice will play. Wine can make you win or make you fail. Buy dry wood and you will burn your pot. If the old is not gone, the new will not come.
A good name is hard to gain but easy to lose. Man may die for gold; bird may die for food. If you don't do bad acts you will fear no harm.

   A bird in the hand is as good as two in the bush. If a man does not keep his word what good is he?

Other Signs and Symbols

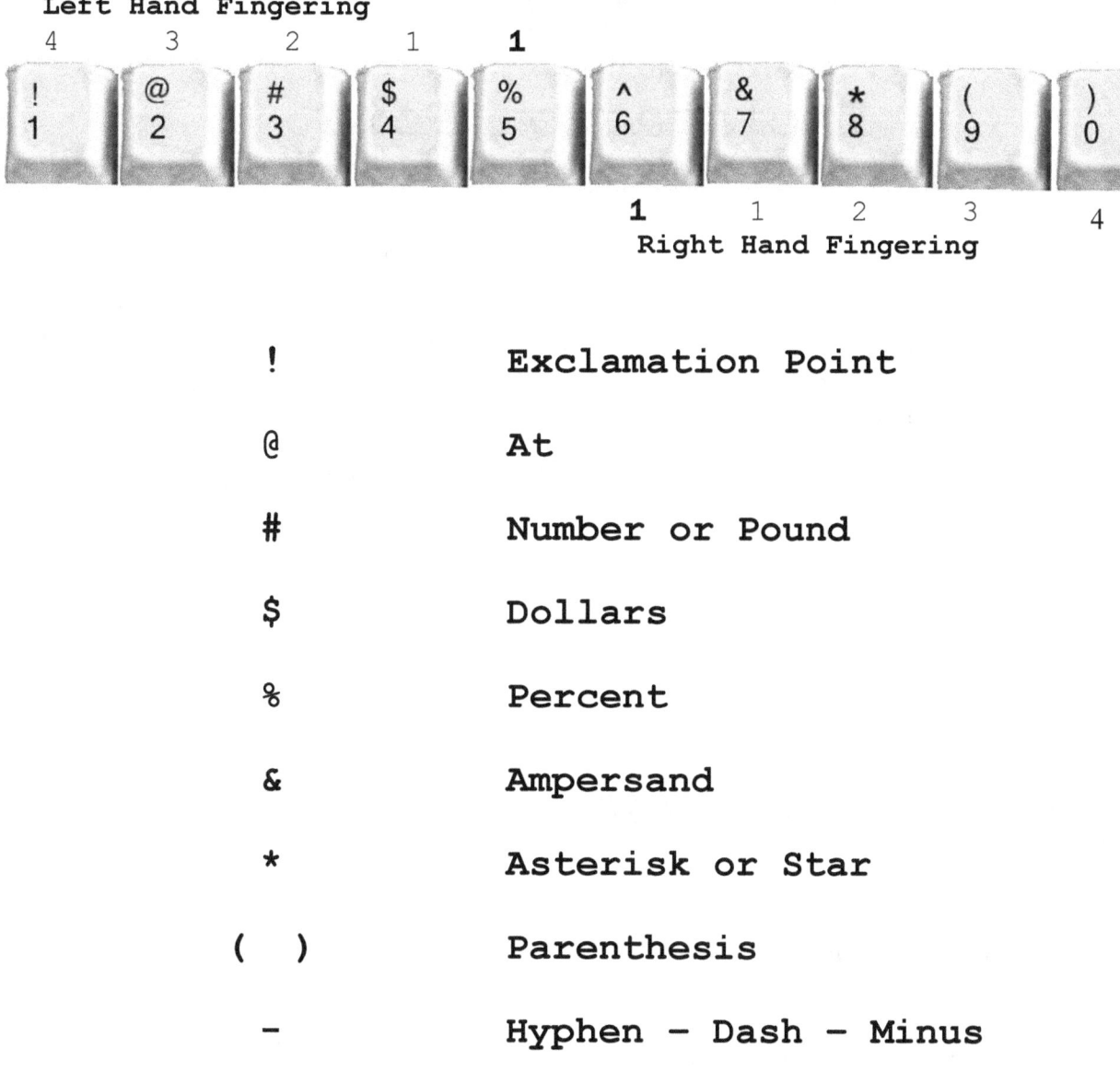

!	Exclamation Point
@	At
#	Number or Pound
$	Dollars
%	Percent
&	Ampersand
*	Asterisk or Star
( )	Parenthesis
-	Hyphen - Dash - Minus
_	Underscore
=	Equal
+	Plus

Exclamation Point

The ! sign is used after a sentence that externalize emotions such as surprise, sensation, outcry, happiness etc. To emphasize or amplify further the above emotions, the exclamation point can be doubled or tripled. Do not space in-between a word and an exclamation point.

Examples :

- → *WOW!*
- → *Help!!*
- → *Happy Birthday!!!*

To produce the !

- *First*, Press and hold down the right side **Shift-key** with the pinky of your right hand;
- *Second*, With the pinky of your left hand, tap the key where there is the **number 1**, it will now produce the !

At

The **@** symbol is used to substitute the words "*at*" and "*at a rate of*" mostly in numerical business accounting; in this case **@** is usually typed among words or numbers with one space before and one after. Also, **@** is the symbol used in computer e-mail addresses, in this case there are no spaces before or after it.

Examples :

- ➔ *I bought 50 boxes of apples @ $20 a box.*
- ➔ *jdoe@trade.com*

To produce the @

- *First*, Press and hold down the right side **Shift-key** with the pinky of your right hand;
- *Second,* With your third finger of your left hand tap the key where there is the **number 2**, it will now produce the **@**

Number or Pound

The # symbol is used in place of the word "*number*", and the word "*pounds*" as a unit of weight. When the # follows a number it is to be read as *pounds*; when it precedes a number it is to be read as *number*. Do not space between the # and the corresponding number.

Examples :

→   *No. 3   or   #3*
→   *50 lbs   or   50#*

To Produce the # :

- *First*, Press and hold down the right side **Shift-key** with the pinky of your right hand;
- *Second*, With your second finger of your left hand tap the key where there is the **number 3**, it will now produce #

Dollar

The $ symbol is used to indicate that the number that follows is an amount of money in dollars. Do not space between the $ and the corresponding amount of money.

Examples :

- →   *$1*   *$10*   *$125*
- →   *$.99*   *(ninety-nine cents of a dollar)*
- →   *$.50*   *(fifty cents of a dollar)*
- →   *$.04*   *(four cents of a dollar)*

To produce the $

- *First*, Press and hold down the right side **Shift-key** with the pinky of your right hand;
- *Second*, With your first finger of your left hand tap the key where there is the **number 4**, it will now produce $

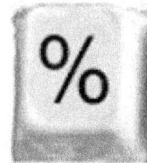

Percent

The **%** symbol is used as a way of expressing a proportion or a fraction in relation to a whole. Do not space between the number and the **%** .

Examples :

→   *1%*   *5%*   *14%*   *100%*

To produce the %

- *First*, Press and hold down the right side **Shift-key** with the pinky of your right hand;
- *Second*, With your first finger (extended) of your left hand tap the key where there is the **number 5**, it will now produce **%**

Ampersand

The **&** symbol is used to substitute the conjunction *"and"* between two names associated as a business entity; and between two proper names and formal titles. In screenplays the **&** symbol indicates a closer partnership than the word "and".

Examples :

- → *Smith **&** Benson*
- → *Lee **&** sons*
- → *The U.S.A. **&** Protector of Guam*
- → *David Spielberg **&** Tom Coppola*

To produce the &

- *First*, Press and hold down the left side **Shift-key** with the pinky of your left hand;
- *Second*, With your first finger of your right hand tap the key where there is the **number 7**, it will now produce **&**

Asterisk or Star

The * symbol is used as *footnote** mark on particular words in a text which directs you to additional explanations about those words at the bottom of the page; as a multiplication sign while using the keyboard; and to put before and after words to emphasize them. Do not space between words and the * ; when the * is used as a multiplication sign type one space before and one after it.

Examples :

→   *footnote*   to mention as a source.*

→   *3 * 3 = 9*

To produce the *

- *First*, Press and hold down the left side **Shift-key** with the pinky of your left hand;
- *Second*, with your second right finger tap the key where there is the **number 8**, it will now produce the *

Parenthesis

The **( )** signs are used to include explanatory remarks, comments or notes in the middle of a sentence; to mark off a joint article in a mathematical operation; and after a number or letter to list points etc. Do not space between the **( )** and the first and last word or number contained in them.

Examples :

- → …..*she was wearing that blouse (the beige one)*…..
- → 5 + 2 *(4 + x)*
- → 1)   2)   3)   4)   5)   etc.

To produce the   ( )

- *First*, Press and hold down the left side **Shift-key** with the pinky of your left hand;
- *Second*, with your third right finger tap the key where there is the **number 9**, it will produce the **(**
- *Third*, Press and hold down the left side **Shift-key** with the pinky of your left hand
- *Fourth*, with your fourth right finger tap the key where there is the **number 0 (zero)** which will now produce the **)**

Hyphen - Dash - Minus

The - symbol is used between the segment of a compound word or name; between the syllables of a word; to replace a comma or parenthesis between words; and as a subtraction sign used for mathematical purposes.

<u>As Hyphen</u>, is used between the two segments of a compound word or name. Do not space before or after this sign.

Examples :

- ➔ *Look-out*
- ➔ *in-law*

<u>As Dash</u>, between words when replacing a comma or parenthesis. Do not space between the - and the first and last word or number contained in them.

Examples :

→ *Just two people in class were absent -Bob and Jim- everyone else was present.*

As Minus, a subtraction sign used for mathematical purposes. Before and after the minus sign type one space.

Examples :

→ *4 - 3 = 1*

To produce the -

- With your fourth finger of your right hand tap the key on the right of the **number 0** key which will produce -

Underscore

The _ is used to make form lines meant to be filled out, such as in: a job application, a doctor file, a contract form, etc. It is also used to replace spacing in e-mail addresses.
Underscore cannot be used to underline.
(To underline words, use the U in the window's formatting toolbar, right above the document you are typing on.)

Examples :

➔ Name: First_____Mid_____Last_____

➔ tim_smith@abc.com

To produce the _

- *First*, Press and hold down with your left hand's pinky the left side **Shift-key;**
- *Second*, With your fourth finger of your right hand tap the key where there is the - **(dash)** , it will now produce _

Equal

The **=** is used for accounting matters or can be used to fill in empty spaces in legal documents (such as a will or a contract) in order to seal the original text content so that no other words can be later added to fraudulently change that document.

Examples :

→ *3 + 2 = 5*

→ *I, Tom Mann declare that all my personal belongings, and all the deposits of my bank accounts and safe deposit box goes to my sister, Esther Mann.==*

To produce the =

- With your fourth right finger simply tap the key where there is the **+ *(plus)*,** it will now produce the **=**

Plus

The + sign is used mostly for math purposes to indicate addition or a positive quantity. Type one space before and one after the + .

Examples :

- → *2 + 2*
- → *12 + 24*
- → *100 + 200*

To produce the +

- *First*, Press and hold down the left side **Shift-key** with the pinky of your left hand;
- *Second*, with your fourth right finger of your right hand tap the key where there is the **= (equal)**, it will now produce the +

Letter Samples

10 letters of different content and format intended for typing practice

PRACTICE INCLUDES THE FOLLOWING FORMATS:

1st *Letter*   Regular 1.0 line spacing

2nd *Letter*   Bolded text

3rd *Letter*   Italicized text

4th *Letter*   Underlined text

5th *Letter*   Indented text

6th *Letter*   Changed line spacing

7th *Letter*   Justified text

8th *Letter*   Bordered text

9th *Letter*   Bulleted list

10th *Letter*   Numbered list

> # Regular 1.0 line spacing

Type the letter free of rhythm in the same format as it appears.

Exercise

Friendly Gardening Program
Golden Gate Park
San Francisco, CA

Dear Friend,

Want to compost? Now's your chance to get started! Our garden program encourages the residents of our county to recycle their plant and food debris with a home compost bin.
Composting is nature's process of recycling organic materials into a rich soil amendment. You can help the environment and get a bargain at the same time with our specially priced, high quality compost bins. These bins will help you recycle leaves, grass clippings, fruit and vegetable trimmings into garden-ready compost. Compost is a nutrient-rich soil amendment that your yard and garden will love.

Sincerely

THIS IS THE STANDARD FORMAT FOR TYPING A LETTER IN MOST INSTANCES WITHOUT THE USE OF ANY FURTHER FORMATTING TO EMPHASIZE POINTS OR EMBELLISH ESTHETICS.

Changed line spacing

Type the letter free of rhythm in the same format as it appears.

Exercise

Dear Adam,

You've been PRE-SELECTED to receive this offer to

lower your interest rate and monthly payment with the

option to get cash out on your home.

Please compare the quoted payment to what you're

currently paying and consider how much you could save

by taking advantage of this program.

THE ENTIRE TEXT IS DOUBLE SPACED,
THE HORIZONTAL SPACING BETWEEN
LINES IS INCREASED, IT MAKES TEXT
EASIER TO READ.

To change the line spacing:
Select the text
Click on Line and Paragraph Spacing
Click on the number of line spaces you want

Bolded text

Type the letter free of rhythm in the same format as it appears.

Exercise

Dear Fellow Taxpayer,

It just doesn't make sense. While our Governor cuts a $3 million program to treat low-income men for prostate cancer, he wants to spend $55 million on a special election that could easily wait until next June. Join me in opposing our Governor's unnecessary special election set for this November.

I have introduced a new bill to cancel his costly November election. With the legislative deadline fast approaching, I need you to send the Governor a message – call off this unnecessary election now and get back to work tackling the real issues facing our state.

THE SECOND PARAGRAPH IS IN BOLD, A TYPE STYLE WITH THICK HEAVY LINES, USED FOR EMPHASIS

To bold text:
    Select the text
    Click on **Bold** *in the* Font *group*

Indented text

Type the letter free of rhythm in the same format as it appears.

Exercise

Dear Member:

It's time to renew your CCC Membership. Like millions of other CCC Members, you know and appreciate the peace of mind that comes with having the best Emergency Road Service around. I'm sure you wouldn't want to be without it for even one day.

> Enclosed please find your new CCC Membership Card. To ensure continuous emergency road service coverage and access to all your CCC Membership benefits, please return the bottom portion of the enclosed statement with your payment in the envelope provided. As long as you remain a CCC Member, we're only a call away when you're in trouble at 1-800-CCC-HELP.

THAT OUTLINED AREA IS CALLED INDENTATION, IT'S USED FOR BLOCK QUOTES OR NESTED PARAGRAPHS

To indent text:
    Select the text
    Click on Increase Indent *in the* Paragraph *group*

Italicized text

Type the letter free of rhythm in the same format as it appears.

Exercise

Dear Mr. Smith,

While you're constantly striving to achieve your personal definition of success, we'd like to recognize you for the attainments you've already achieved.

You're pre-approved for the American Reward Card and for you, there's no annual fee for the first year. You should know that pre-approval status is not easily achieved. But with your excellent financial record, our decision was really very simple – we want you as a Card Member. In fact, we value your Card membership enough to offer you the Card fee-free for the first year. Plus, you can share the benefits of Card membership with someone you know through an additional Card –also fee-free for the first year.

THE SECOND PARAGRAPH IS IN *ITALICS*, A TYPE STYLE WITH CHARACTERS THAT SLANT TO THE RIGHT, USED FOR EMPHASIS

To italicize text:
    Select the text
    Click on Italic *in the* Font *group*

Justified text

Type the letter free of rhythm in the same format as it appears.

Exercise

Dear Frequent Flyer:

I'm writing to share some exciting news. As of January 25, 2006, you have 21,000 Airmiles in your account. Now you can add as many as 15,000 more Airmiles for a total of 36,000 by accepting the Gold Alpha Airmiles Credit Card from USA Wings.
Think of it -in addition to receiving 15,000 bonus miles after your very first purchase, you can pick up 2,500 more bonus miles simply by adding an Additional Card member, fee-free, to your account. What's more, you can earn at least one mile for each eligible dollar spent on both cards, so miles can add up fast.

THE ENTIRE TEXT IS JUSTIFIED, JUSTIFY IS THE ALIGNMENTOF THE LEFT AND RIGHT SIDES OF THE TEXT WITH THE MARGINS IN ORDER TO MAKE TEXT EASIER TO READ.

To justify text:
Select the text
Click on Justify *in the* Paragraph *group*

Numbered list

Type the letter free of rhythm in the same format as it appears.

Exercise

Dear Harry,

I'd like to make you an offer I think and hope you'll find irresistible.
I'd like to send you:

1. A sample issue of Customer Reports ($4.99 at the news stand).

2. A free copy of the Customer Reports Buying Guide 2006(regularly $9.99) with hundredsbrand name product ratings.

3. A bonus Flip-Top Calculator. This novel design easily fits into a pocket or purse, for use in the home, office and on shopping trips.

THE LIST ABOVE IS NUMBERED, NUMBERED LISTS CONTAINS ITEMS THAT ARE NUMBERED, and IT'S USED TO ARRANGE ITEMS IN A CERTAIN ORDER.

To number a list:
Select the text
Click on Numbering *in the* Paragraph *group*

Bulleted list

Type the letter free of rhythm in the same format as it appears.

Exercise

Dear Consumer,

Now you can earn a rebate on your gas bill with our gas saving program. Due to cold weather, short supplies, and natural gas costs in our state are increasing as much as 40% this winter. With this gas savings program, when you reduce your gas usage from January through March, you'll receive a rebate.
Gas saving tips:
- Turn your thermostat 5-10 degrees below where you typically set it, and further at night.
- Seal leaks in heating ducts and around windows.
- Set water heater at 120 degrees or medium.
- Install energy-saving showerheads and faucet aerators. Wash your clothes in cold water.

THE LIST ABOVE IS BULLETED, BULLETED LISTS CONTAINS ITEMS THAT ARE BULLETED, ITS USED TO ARRANGE ITEMS WITH NO SPECIFIC ORDER.

To bullet a list:
    Select the text
    Click on Bullets *in the* Paragraph *group*

Bordered text

Type the letter free of rhythm in the same format as it appears.

Exercise

```
Dear Donor,

We need small household items and your usable
clothes. Donations are tax deductible. Place your
bags or boxes curbside clearly visible from the
street by 8:00AM on Thursday January 26. Attach this
letter to your donation! Our truck will pick up your
donation between 8:00 AM and 5:00 PM rain or shine!
Our truck will be on your street. No need to call
unless you live in a gated community or have special
instructions -Donation Service Line:
1-800-CHARITY.
```

THE ENTIRE TEXT IS BORDERED, THE TEXT IS BORDERED WHEN IT IS BOXED WITH LINES, ITS USED ESTHETICALLY TO CREATE AN ATTRACTIVE PAGE LAYOUT.

To border text:
    Select the text
    Click on Outside Border *in the* Paragraph *group*

Underlined text

Type the letter free of rhythm in the same format as it appears.

Exercise

Dear Homeowner:

Halfmoon Roofing has put on over 7,000 roofs in our area. If you are considering having any roofing work done please give us a call or check us out on the web at www.halfmoon.com. If you are going to re-roof in the next year, pricing will be lower in the winter months.
During the winter, people do not think about roofing due to the weather. However, there are many weeks when the weather is great and we keep busy by offering lower pricing.

<u>Take advantage of the seasonal nature of the roofing business.</u>

<u>UNDERLINED</u>, A TYPE STYLE WITH A LINE DRAWN UNDERNEATH THE TEXT, USED FOR EMPHASIS.

To underline text:
Select the text
Click on <u>Underline</u> *in the* Font *group*

Table of Roman Numerals

All the Roman Numerals can be graphically made with the use of only 7 letters of the alphabet in uppercase: I, V, X, L, C, D, M. Roman numerals do not include the number zero.

$$I = 1$$

$$V = 5$$

$$X = 10$$

$$L = 50$$

$$C = 100$$

$$D = 500$$

$$M = 1000$$

The combination of any of the above numerals will make any other needed number.

II = 2	III = 3	IV = 4	DX = 510
VII = 7	VIII = 8	IX = 9	DC = 600
XVII = 17	XXVIII = 28	XXXIX = 39	MD = 1500

A bigger numeral in front of a smaller numeral equals the sum of both numerals.

Roman	Modern
V + I = VI	5 + 1 = 6
X + I = XI	10 + 1 = 11
L + I = LI	50 + 1 = 51
L + V = LV	50 + 5 = 55

A smaller numeral in front of a bigger numeral equals the difference of the bigger numeral and the smaller numeral.

Roman	Modern
V – I = IV	5 – 1 = 4
X – I = IX	10 – 1 = 9
L – V = VL	50 – 5 = 45
L – X = XL	50 – 10 = 40
C – L = LC	100 – 50 = 50
C – X = XC	100 – 10 = 90

Two equal numerals equal the sum of both numerals.

Roman	Modern
X + X = XX	10 + 10 = 20
C + C = CC	100 + 100 = 200
M + M = MM	1000 + 1000 = 2000

Frequently Asked Questions About This Book

- *For who was this book was made for and why?*

This book was made to give solid typing foundations to beginner typists of any age, and to solidify the *Touch-typing* technique of any intermediate level typist.

- *How are the exercises in this book structured?*

All the exercises in this book are designed to bring the student, gradually, from the level of typing looking back and forth between the words of the text and the letters on the keyboard, to the realm of *Touch-typing* where the student will be typing looking only at the text.

- *Why the use of the different sizes of letters for the printing of the exercises in this book?*

The four different sizes of letters are use for **rhythmic** reasons because the author's technical necessity to graphically represent the four different speeds in which the letters in the exercises will be practiced.

- *Does the student have to type the letters using the four different sizs?*

No, absolutely not. The four different sizes used for the printing of the exercises in this book are exclusively to show to the student how the letters have to be practiced in their four different speeds. For maximum clarity, the student should type all of the letters and words in **size 20 Microsoft San Serif font**.

- *Do I have to practice an exercise or a lesson just once?*

No, you can practice a line of exercise or an entire lesson as many times as you feel or need to, just do it always as specified: orderly and with the due rhythm.

- *Why use size 20 font to do the typing practices?*

Because size 20 letters appear with the right visual consistency, not to small, not to big, quite comfortable for the beginner typist to visually follow on the monitor.

- *What kind of more advanced typing practice can I do after having mastered the exercises in this book?*

For more advanced typing practice, simply type down the text from the mail that you receive daily. You may be amazed how much your typing technique can improve by just typing down the original content and format of letters, documents and promotional advertising sent to you by the variety of business establishments on the market.

LITTLE DICTIONARY

1ˢᵗ Lesson

FALL	……	to go straight down under force of gravity
GALL	……	feeling of ill will
HALL	……	an enclosed passage way

2ⁿᵈ Lesson

FLAG	……	a rectangular piece of flat fabric that is used as a symbol
DRAG	……	to pull slowly
SHAG	……	a bushy tangled mass or covering

3ʳᵈ Lesson

FLEE	……	to run away from
GLEE	……	joy
FREE	……	not ruled by another

4ᵗʰ Lesson

FOIL	……	to keep someone from his desire
SOIL	……	the upper layer of Earth on which plants grow
TOIL	……	working hard

5ᵗʰ Lesson

FLAW	……	a small often hidden defect
DRAW	……	to cause to come out of a container
THAW	……	to pass from the solid to the liquid state

6th Lesson

FLIP	……	types of gymnastic moves
DRIP	……	to release liquid in tiny amounts
QUIP	……	a short humorous statement

7th Lesson

FILE	……	to enter on public record or legal record
RILE	……	to irritate or anger
TILE	……	roofing materials

8th Lesson

DANK	……	unpleasantly wet
RANK	……	someone's position
YANK	……	to pull up by the roots

9th Lesson

DOOM	……	fateful determination in advance
ROOM	……	a space that is or may be occupied by something
ZOOM	……	to go up rapidly

10th Lesson

DING	……	a high pitched sound made by striking a metallic or glass object
KING	……	the head of the kingdom
ZING	……	liveliness of spirit

11th Lesson

DAMP	......	lightly touched with water
VAMP	......	to return something to working order
CAMP	......	a site of temporary outdoor shelter

12th Lesson

SASS	......	back-talk
MASS	......	the quality of being heavy
BASS	......	a low pitch deep sound

13th Lesson

RAGE	......	violent and uncontrolled anger
WAGE	......	cash payment for work
PAGE	......	a sheet of paper

14th Lesson

SIDE	......	the space immediately next to someone or something
HIDE	......	to put something out of sight
RIDE	......	to be conveyed in a vehicle

15th Lesson

SLAM	......	to shut violently and noisily
SCAM	......	a deceptive act or operation
EXAM	......	a testing of student's knowledge

16th Lesson

FRAY	......	fight, struggle
STAY	......	to continue to be at certain place
AWAY	......	in a direction parting from this place

17th Lesson

AJAR	......	partially opened
STAR	......	a self-luminous, celestial mass of gas
CZAR	......	a king or emperor

18th Lesson

GOOP	......	an ill-mannered person
LOOP	......	simple closed curves
POOP	......	the back deck of a ship

19th Lesson

GAIN	......	to come into possession of
VAIN	......	lacking substance or worth
RAIN	......	water-droplets falling from the sky

20th Lesson

JACK	......	any of several devices replacing human labor
HACK	......	gain unauthorized access to a computer
SACK	......	to loot or pillage – a large bag of strong coarse material

21st Lesson

JADE	......	gems
FADE	......	to become less intense
WADE	......	to walk in or through water

22nd Lesson

KILL	......	to take a life
FILL	......	to make full or load completely
DILL	......	an aromatic herb

23rd Lesson

LICE	......	any parasitic biting or blood-sucking insect
VICE	......	substituting for; acting in place of; and replace
NICE	......	easy to get along with

24th Lesson

PUFF	......	to produce an ingoing current of air or smoke
CUFF	......	a band of fabric attached to the wrist
BUFF	......	to rub a surface in order to make it shine

25th Lesson

HARD	......	not easy to do
BARD	......	someone who composes and recites poems
YARD	......	a unit of length in both the US system and the British system

www.ingramcontent.com/pod-product-compliance
Lightning Source LLC
Chambersburg PA
CBHW080243180526
45167CB00006B/2401